CHARITY MANAGEMENT

Britain faces challenges that weren't imaginable thirty years ago, challenges which charities, rooted as they are in community action and the public good, should be ideally suited to tackle. But the charity sector seems paralysed. Even after a decade of cuts and immense social and environmental disruption charities are still fighting hard to maintain business as usual. To develop new responses to our changing world the charity sector desperately needs to reinvent itself, radically re-engaging with communities and developing powerful and scalable responses to the challenges facing the UK in the coming decades. What are the ties that bind charities, rendering them unable to re-invent themselves and to re-imagine their services, even when they face existential crises?

This book explores how charities in the UK really operate, as seen through the eyes of people who work in and with charities, and investigates what holds charities back from change. It demonstrates what we can learn from entrepreneurship and market disruption in the private sector, and points to ways in which the sector can re-imagine what it does and how it does this. It presents a new ambition for charities to break free of their history and imagine a new role for themselves in shaping the future for our society.

Presenting a new ambition for charities to imagine a new role for themselves in shaping the future for our society, this volume is especially valuable for academics and professionals in the fields of charity and non-profit management, organisational change, and strategic management.

Sarah Mitchell is Chief Executive of Cycling UK and Vice Chair of the Nationwide Foundation.

CHARITY AND NON-PROFIT STUDIES

Series Editors: Paul Palmer and Peter Grant

Demystifying Social Finance and Social Investment
Mark Salway with Jim Clifford, Paul Palmer, Peter Grant

Charity Management
Leadership, Evolution, and Change
Sarah Mitchell

CHARITY MANAGEMENT

Leadership, Evolution, and Change

Sarah Mitchell

Routledge
Taylor & Francis Group

NEW YORK AND LONDON

First published 2022
by Routledge
605 Third Avenue, New York, NY 10158

and by Routledge
2 Park Square, Milton Park, Abingdon, Oxon OX14 4RN

Routledge is an imprint of the Taylor & Francis Group, an informa business

Library of Congress Cataloging-in-Publication Data
Names: Mitchell, Sarah, 1975- author.
Title: Charity management : leadership, evolution, and change / Sarah Mitchell.
Description: 1 Edition. | New York : Routledge, 2021. |
Series: Charity and non-profit studies | Includes bibliographical references and index.
Identifiers: LCCN 2021002591 (print) | LCCN 2021002592 (ebook) |
ISBN 9780367687946 (hardback) | ISBN 9780367687960 (paperback) |
ISBN 9781003139089 (ebook)
Subjects: LCSH: Charities–Management. | Nonprofit organizations–Management. | Organizational change.
Classification: LCC HV41 .M498 2021 (print) | LCC HV41 (ebook) |
DDC 361.7068–dc23
LC record available at https://lccn.loc.gov/2021002591
LC ebook record available at https://lccn.loc.gov/2021002592

ISBN: 978-0-367-68794-6 (hbk)
ISBN: 978-0-367-68796-0 (pbk)
ISBN: 978-1-003-13908-9 (ebk)

DOI: 10.4324/9781003139089

Typeset in Bembo
by Taylor & Francis Books

For Dil, Mel and Andrew.

CONTENTS

ILLUSTRATIONS

ACKNOWLEDGEMENTS

A great many people have helped with the development of this book over many years and it isn't possible to list them all here. Thank you to the board of trustees at Heart of the City, who supported this concept from the start, in particular to Sir Harvey McGrath, Sushil Saluja, Anthony Impey but also to Linda Barnard, Rob Powell, Rachel Engel, Carmen Whitelock, Arjan van den Berkmortel, Fiona Clark, Nick Turner and Giles French. The team at the Centre for Charity Effectiveness at City Business School have been extremely generous with their time and feedback and have made this book possible, in particular Peter Grant and Paul Palmer, but also Alex Skailes, Mark Salway, Stephen Lee and Rob Compton – thank you! Thanks also to Dan Howard and Janet Atherton at Cycling UK for supporting me in the final stages of this book.

For their incredibly valuable and thought-provoking insights, feedback and views I am very grateful to Ali Bateman, Alison Katerji, Anthony Harte, Beth Breeze, Boris Pomroy, Caroline Lien, Carolyn Housman, Dan Corry, Duncan Shrubsole, Emma Walsh, James Blake, Janet Thorne, Jon Sparkes, Judith McNeil, Kate Pieroudis, Kristina Glenn, Mark Atkinson, Mary Rose Gunn, Michelle Hill, Penny Lawrence, Penny Wilson, Steve Griffiths and Tunde Banjoko.

Thanks above all to Andrew Glazzard without whose conviction that this book needed to be written, and by me, it might never have seen the light of day, and to Dil Mitchell for being my number one reader.

INTRODUCTION

When thinking about a career, I, like many others, have always had an ambition to make a positive difference to society. Also, like many people, I had a somewhat vague idea of what that meant. In my case it led, by a slightly meandering route, into working first in politics and then in charities, working my way up from volunteer and junior roles to becoming a trustee and a charity chief executive. Through my career I have worked in, and with, a variety of large and small charities and met some incredible, fascinating and wonderful people. I have also had opportunities to work outside the sector and to reflect on charities from a different perspective. Increasingly I have asked myself and others questions about our sector, about what we are doing and why. Two questions in particular have plagued me: are we really making a significant difference? How could we do better?

In writing this book I became aware of how nervous we are as a sector of asking ourselves these sorts of questions. More than one of my interviewees cautioned me against being too challenging, for fear of creating enemies in the sector. Several of my interviewees asked to be anonymised in this book for the same reason. I understand this defensiveness in a sector which has experienced a barrage of criticism over recent years and which is beset by unachievable and often mutually conflicting expectations. My motivation to write this book though is very far from wanting to join the chorus of critics.

I wanted to write this book out of a strong feeling of commitment to, and affection for, the charity sector. I believe charities have an essential role to play in shaping society and I think that they have strengths that are peculiarly well suited to the technological, social and political changes we are experiencing. However, the world is changing quickly around us, and over recent years I have been painfully aware, through my own experience, of the challenges facing charities in adapting and responding to this pace of change. In this book my aim was to explore how charities can shape their work to exploit these emerging opportunities, and to understand why this development has been so difficult for many charities to do so far.

My experience has made me aware of how the myriad different expectations about charities bind charity leaders. Charity leaders can feel paralysed by the contradictory expectations of our funders, public, staff, trustees, and of ourselves. These contradictions can make us feel as if it is impossible to get anything right. Moving forwards and tackling future challenges requires more freedom and agency than the sector has at present. I wanted to question these ties that bind us.

In order to explore this I have structured the book's chapters around some of the issues that I have seen holding charities back. These often relate to confused and conflicting expectations about what a charity is and what activities it should undertake; how we measure its effectiveness; how charities are, and should be, funded; how charities are managed; whether charities should be run by volunteers or paid staff and how they are governed. In each of these chapters I try to give some insights into the variety of ways that charities tackle these challenges today and to show how these impact a charity's ability to adapt and be effective in a rapidly changing external environment. Towards the end of the book I explore examples of organisations (not necessarily charities) that have overcome some of the hurdles faced by charities. These are not intended to be exemplars, but to be illustrative of the attitude, culture and structures that might enable the charities of the future to ensure that they continue to be relevant.

Methodology

For this book I have focused on charities that employ staff (inevitably these are larger charities) and those which campaign and deliver services, as they are likely to be those most recognisable to the public as charities. These are also the charities with which I am most familiar. There are of course many very large grant-making charities (e.g. the Wellcome Trust) and culture and heritage organisations (e.g. the National Gallery), which I do not focus on here but I would be very interested to read about the experiences and expectations of those working in these very different types of charity.

I am not an academic and so the approach of this book has not been that of a typical doctorate. I undertook an organic literature review for each of the areas covered by my chapters which was supplemented by the recommendations of the team of experts at the City Business School Centre for Charity Effectiveness. I held a series of semi-structured interviews with people from within and around the charity sector between December 2019 and December 2020. These interviews were framed by the central questions of the book's chapters.

An Operational View

It was important to me to write this book about the sector from an operational perspective. The experiences of those working day to day in UK charities are rarely heard beyond the sector and I believe that the complexity and challenges of their roles are little understood.

As I am not an academic, the academic research papers on the sector, which I read for the first time when planning this book, surprised me. There are relatively few papers, and the vast majority of those that do exist seem skewed towards fundraising and focus on US charities. Very few of the papers spoke to me of my experience in the sector. I have used academic and think-tank research for this book, alongside newspaper reports. I have relied heavily on the excellent Civil Society Almanac produced annually by NCVO. I have also, crucially, drawn on the experiences of interviewees who lead charities and/or are experts on the sector.

Throughout the book I have utilised research evidence as far as possible, but inevitably this book will present a partial view: my work has been predominantly in service delivery and campaigning charities, in London or nationally, and my contacts are not, and do not attempt to be, representative of a sector that is immensely diverse. Throughout the book I draw on my own experience because I believe that these insights are useful, a sort of 'lived experience' of the sector, to borrow one of our current popular phrases. However, I appreciate that I offer only one point of view and I welcome hearing other perspectives, as we all should. Above all this book is intended to open a debate, to encourage colleagues across the sector and beyond to ask ourselves more searching questions about what we do, and why, and how we can do more and do in better in the decades to come.

1

WHAT IS CHARITY TODAY?

What is charity today? Is it the slightly tatty community hall down the road or the Tate Gallery? Is it the group of volunteer parents who run your local kids football club, or the envelope that came through your door with the picture of the hungry-looking child on the outside and a free pen inside? Is it the retired people who run your local Oxfam shop or the software developers designing new products to support vulnerable young people?

Charity is all of these things and more. It is where we imagine it to be, located in rundown buildings with erratic opening hours, but also on state-of-the-art websites with adverts that track our online preferences. It's delivered by well-off older people who want to 'give something back' and it's a place of work for many. It's about disabled people, it's about pets, it's about the natural environment, it's about sport. The sheer variety of charity is sometimes bewildering but it's also inspiring. This is not a state-mandated area where people are corralled into specific activities, but the creation of a charity is the spontaneous and personal realisation of an urge to make a difference. Taking a step back from the sector I have worked in for more than 15 years it is astonishing to behold – all those people, all those causes, all over the country.

But this very variety presents a challenge. All these different charities bring with them many different and often conflicting sets of expectations. These expectations come in the form of explicit regulations and funder requirements, but they are also implicit in the minds of donors, the public, charity workers and volunteers. These expectations have evolved over many years and some are out of date. In this book I will explore how these expectations mesh with the reality for charities in the 2020s and how they hold us back from anticipating the challenges of the coming decades.

DOI: 10.4324/9781003139089-1

Alternate Reality

The gulf between the reality of the charity sector and public perceptions is wide, as Penny Wilson, CEO of Getting on Board, told me:

> The public has many misconceptions about the charity sector, about its size and complexity and heterogeneity, about CEO salaries. Also, the government doesn't always recognise charities' enormous contribution to society, as we've seen in their response to the sector's calls for support during the Covid-19 crisis.
>
> *(Wilson 2020)*

The traditional and enduring view of charity derives from its origins. Evolving out of a religious concept of 'caritas,' Latin for 'caring,' charity was originally conceived of as an action to benefit another without the aim of getting anything in return. Over the centuries this evolved into a sector that now complements and compensates for gaps in the services supplied by the state and the private sector (Dees 2012).

There are around 167,000 charities in the UK today. They employed 909,088 people in 2019 and work with a further 19 million volunteers each year (NCVO 2020). Charities come in all shapes and sizes and pinning down a definition has vexed academics for many years (Alcock 2010). 'Charities', 'non-profits', 'the third sector' or 'civil society' – each of these groups include a subtly different bundle of organisations but each tends to be defined more by what they are not (they are not private businesses, they are not the state, they do not distribute profit), than what they actually are. As Nicholas Deakin wrote in his 1996 *Report of the Commission on the Future of the Voluntary Sector*:

> There is no single "authentic" voluntary sector for which a simple master plan can be drawn up.
>
> *(Alcock 2010: 7)*

Most attempts to define the sector reveal surprising overlaps with both the private sector and the public sector. Peter Grant of City Business School's Centre for Charity Effectiveness describes this as a continuum of sorts, with the most traditional, altruistic charity at one end and the most rapacious, profit-driven company at the other. Along this continuum both charities and businesses would locate themselves according to their degree of social responsibility or altruism, and so we'd see a clustering of 'business like' charities running trading companies or contracts around the middle, alongside B-Corps like Patagonia or mutuals like the Nationwide Building Society or John Lewis (Grant 2020).

If we narrow our focus, as I do in this book, to UK-registered charities, most have some core founding elements in common. Charities are created by private actors, but they are set up to deliver work that must benefit the public (and which would perhaps not otherwise be undertaken); they may have the ability to reach groups that government, private sector and the state cannot, or do not; and they are run through a more diffuse power structure than other organisations, which gives their stake-holders – service users, volunteers, trustees, workers, donors – more agency and involvement. This creates a very different culture and a distinct set of expectations. As Noel Hyndman puts it:

> charities are very different from businesses. They have missions other than to make money. Funding comes from donors who provide funds with no expec-tation of direct economic benefit to themselves. Recipients of goods and services often have no ability to pay or seek an alternative provider. Charities rely heavily on trust relationships and communal accountability, rather than market rela-tionships and contractual accountability.
>
> *(Hyndman 2017)*

However, as well as being culturally distinct from the business sector, charities are also very different from one another. Charities today work across an enormously wide range of areas, but they also do their work in increasingly diverse ways. This wide-ranging sector isn't necessarily visible to the general public. Charities don't talk about themselves as a sector but only as individual organisations, and they lack the spokespeople to represent them, as Dan Corry, CEO of New Philanthropy Capital advised me. Each charity CEO represents her or his own cause, and charity mem-bership organisations such as NCVO or ACEVO are, hidebound by their members' diverse interests, limited to speaking in generalities (Corry 2020). The diversity of charities makes it difficult for anything specific to be said about the sector as a whole, either in defence or in criticism. The fact that any point cannot be held to be true across this vast 'loose and baggy monster' (Bryson et al. 2002) may have contributed to the slow pace of change across the charity sector. When no single improvement, change or solution can be identified, which does not have a negative consequence for other parts of the same sector, there is a risk of inertia within the charity sector itself and from funders and government.

A Thousand Flowers Blooming

Charities are set up by highly motivated citizens or groups of citizens, and they spring up organically. They are not planned or coordinated and they are not required to be a logical response to objectively defined need. Nevertheless, whether or not their work corresponds to the areas of greatest social need, governments in general recognise the value of charity. The reasons for this are subject to much debate, but include the idea that charities complement state provision by piloting innovative interventions, as well as the idea that charity models the positive engagement of citizens as volunteers and as agents in solving social issues rather than relying on the state to intervene. Govern-ments may also welcome the additional resource that charities can bring, potentially reducing the burden on the state and taxes (Dees 2012; Davies 2016).

The regulation of charities in the UK has signalled an attempt to harness the power of citizens' urge to philanthropy by nudging this gently towards generating genuine 'public good.' The Charity Commissioners Board was first appointed in 1853 in an early attempt at formal supervision of UK charities, but it wasn't until the 1960s that government introduced the first comprehensive charities act, which required all charities to be registered. Only as recently as 2006 was a statutory definition of charity set out in more detail and for the first time required charities to pass the public benefit test (House of Lords 2017).

Today all registered charities in England and Wales are regulated by the Charity Commission, in Scotland the Office of the Scottish Charity Regulator fulfils this function and in Northern Ireland it is the Charity Commission for Northern Ireland. Charities across the UK have to follow the rules set out by their national regulator, on the way they are governed and also on the broad types of work that they do. In exchange, registered charities are exempt from corporation tax on any surpluses they make (though they still pay VAT and national insurance), they can apply to receive Gift Aid on individual donations and (depending on their local government) reductions in business rates. Registered charities also enjoy a sort of accredited status: many grant funders will only fund registered charities, seeing this as a mark of quality which gives them comfort that their money is indeed going to a good cause.

There are, then, significant incentives to become a registered charity, but the government does expect something in return. The *quid pro quo* is that the work that registered charities do must provide a public benefit. Unlike businesses, which might be purpose-driven by choice alongside their profit-making objectives, charities are required by law to put public benefit above all other considerations. This makes common sense – after all, the public would expect a children's cancer charity to put children with cancer at the heart of what it does. If the charity also happens to benefit others (e.g. by giving some positive PR to a company that has sponsored one of its events), this has to be an incidental by-product of its main aim, which should always be to help children with cancer.

Public benefit is a fairly vague concept and today there are 13 different types of public benefit under which a charity may register. These range from the "prevention or relief of poverty" and "advancement of health or saving lives", to "advancement of religion", to "promotion of the efficiency of the armed forces of the Crown, or of the efficiency of the police, fire and rescue services or ambulance services"(Charity Commission 2013).

As these broad definitions indicate, the type of work that charities do is still incredibly varied. Within the field of social services alone, charities run children's day care centres, supplementary schools, adoption services, child development centres, foster care, nurseries, parent education classes, single parent agencies and domestic violence refuges. Charities run an overwhelming array of services supporting people with disabilities, such as by providing transport services (community buses), employment and education services, independent living and leisure support, in-home services for older people, home meals services, nutrition classes, support groups, personal counselling and credit counselling/money management services. In the UK and overseas, charities provide disaster and emergency prevention and response including volunteer fire departments, lifeboat services, air ambulance services, temporary shelters, emergency and temporary housing, food and clean water, clothing, education, emergency cash assistance, and furniture. UK charities do everything from digging artesian wells in Afghanistan to providing food banks in Bolton.

The sheer range of what charities deliver all around us is astounding, and the Charity Commission's categories of public benefit seem all-encompassing. But they do conceal some surprising anomalies. One of the most controversial areas is the inclusion of private schools, which qualify as charities under the "advancement of education". This is despite the fact that evidence shows that private education perpetuates inequality and suppresses social mobility in the UK (Green, Anders, Henderson and Henseke 2017).

By contrast, some community-based non-profit organisations are not able to register. The community-based organisation where I was a trustees for eight years, CFPT, supported private tenants in slum rentals in a highly disadvantaged area of Camden. It survived on a shoestring of grant income, but it did not qualify to register as a charity (despite repeated attempts). This was because not all private tenants are necessarily disadvantaged – even though the ones we worked with were suffering severe health and financial problems as a direct result of their tenancy type. As a result this organisation (total annual income £65,000), which is registered instead under the Co-operative and Community Benefit Societies Act 2014, is excluded from applying to the majority of grant funders. Nor does it enjoy the tax breaks that are enjoyed by, say, Eton College (income £50,900,000 in 2018) or the Sidmouth Donkey Sanctuary (income £42,000,000 in 2018).

So, not all non-profits are registered charities and not all registered charities are what we might expect to be charities. However, for the purpose of this book I will focus on registered charities because these are the sub-sector that the government is explicitly encouraging through regulation. Later, I will explore whether alternative forms of constitution may offer more flexibility for organisations to respond to the changing world around us.

Change is Coming

For more than ten years the charity sector has been telling itself that change is coming. First the financial crash, then years of government cuts, governance scandals like that of Kids Company and safeguarding scandals such as that which consumed Oxfam, immense advances in technology, dramatic shifts of emotion in identity politics – all have changed the context in which charities operate. But seemingly little in the charity sector itself has changed. We still have a broadly similar number of registered charities and they work on broadly similar areas. What's more, the same charities dominate. As Sir Harvey McGrath, Chair of Big Society Capital and major UK philanthropist, told me:

In the business world new entrants would push out incumbents, as the market drives innovation in products and services. But this doesn't happen so much in the third sector. Often charities seem to suffer from inertia, perhaps due to the lack of these 'market pressures', and to a combination of governance issues and funding challenges

(McGrath 2020).

Now, in 2021, the Covid-19 pandemic has forced a break with the past like no other challenge in living memory. Charities have been jolted out of their usual rhythm and now find themselves able to deliver their work in ways they had never considered possible. However, the question I'm most concerned with in this book is whether this situation can, and will, bring about the sort of shift in thinking that the sector needs, in order to prepare itself and its people for the rapid changes we anticipate in the coming decades.

So, what are these changes likely to be? One of the rare pieces of work exploring the medium to long-term outlook for the charity sector finds that shifts in demography, technology, funding and volunteer support are the key trends that will influence the charity sector in the developed world (Cordery et al. 2017). Peter Grant identifies two themes that have dominated my conversations with charity leaders:

Climate change and digitisation. That's not just about getting a website set up, but also digitisation as an issue in itself: where should charities intervene in the digital debate? Recognising the importance of challenging indoctrination and exploitation online and protecting personal data.

(Grant 2020)

The disruption caused by Covid-19 shouldn't distract us from these long-term tectonic shifts. But are charities willing and able to respond to these dramatic changes?

The Myth of Adaptability

This book will explore many widely held myths and assumptions about the sector: one of these is that charities are distinctively innovative and responsive. I confess that I've stated on plenty of funding applications that charities are *adaptable, fleet of foot, agile*. The House of Lords took this view too, in its 2017 Select Committee report:

We are living through a time of profound economic, social and technological change and the environment in which charities are working is altering dramatically. We do not believe that this is a temporary aberration: such disruptive changes are likely to become the norm. Charities have always helped society through periods of upheaval. We are confident they will do so again

(House of Lords 2017: 3).

However, the more I have discussed these assumptions with colleagues in charities, the less certain I am that this is actually true. This point about adaptation is one that I will return to again and again in this book. In my experience charities are by their very nature subject to enormous forces that lie outside their control. This state of being buffeted by constant change results from charities' peculiar position, operating in the undefined gap between the state, the communities we live in, and the private sector. The environment in which charities operate is to a large extent at the mercy of these other sectors, how they operate and interrelate.

For example, when the state introduced benefits sanctions and long waits for Universal Credit payments ensued for those in urgent need, charity food banks run by the Trussell Trust stepped in to feed vulnerable people; where private companies emerged as competitors to deliver social care contracts, charities such as the carers charity I led, Carers Network, found themselves having to re-configure their work in unit costs; and where shifts in society meant families living further apart, charities like SharedLives Plus stepped in to provide support for older people, which might traditionally have been supplied by local family members. The actions of these other sectors can put pressure on charities to re-think both what they do and how they do it.

It is clear to see that new charities do sometimes emerge to fill these emerging gaps, and existing charities do regularly respond to these external forces and make tweaks to their work in order to survive. However, I think it is important to make a distinction between these tactical shifts, in response to inconvenient changes in the external world, and innovation which takes a medium to long-term view about a charity's work as a whole and develops a longer term, strategic response.

Disruption caused by long-term changes to the world around us is not just something that charities need to put up with and tweak their service around, it's something anyone working in the sector needs to learn to embrace. However, charity employees are just like everyone else: they get change-fatigue and they get attached to the projects they have poured their energy and hopes into. And it is fair to say that the sector has, over the last ten years, been subjected to change that has been so unpredictable and so far-reaching that most charities find themselves simply focused on survival.

Survival for charities constantly requires small alterations in what we do, but this tends to manifest itself in these tactical, short-term tweaks I describe above. It is charities being forced to adapt under duress in response to urgent issues. It means fire-fighting. It doesn't mean thoughtful, considered adaptation with a 10- to 20-year time horizon. If you were to ask any charity CEO where they plan their charity to be in 10 to 20 years I expect you'd get a bemused smile (this is a very polite sector). An experienced and very well-connected grant funder told me in 2019 that none of the major charities she knew well were really planning for the future: their focus instead was on "preserving business as usual". This corresponds to Julia Unwin's description of the widespread phenomenon of the 'starved organisation' which is so overwhelmed it becomes unable to develop or to devise new solutions to problems (Unwin 2004).

I have heard similar responses to the Covid-19 pandemic. As charities have haemorrhaged cash, their response has been to cut back and buckle down, preserving essential existing services but delivering them online. Although early surveys have heralded an increase in innovation, on closer inspection this is (at the time of writing) being used to describe the provision of short-term crisis-response services (such as the excellent work delivering food and medical supplies to those who were shielding and those suffering significant loss of income) and use of new software and hardware to adapt to remote working (CAF 2020).

This focus on preserving business as usual as far as possible is understandable given the state of the sector. Crises push leaders to focus on the here and now; volatility presents the illusion that planning is pointless and most of us, when focused on survival, lack the time and headspace to think about the future and to think strategically. As Charles Handy argued in *The Second Curve*, when "income, productivity or reputation is falling it is hard to contemplate anything new" (Handy 2015 cited in Smith 2019: 278).

But this is not the mindset of 'innovative' and 'adaptable' organisations. It is also a warning sign for the charity sector's ability to deliver services that are capable of meeting the future needs of our societies, where there may no longer be a *business as usual* option. If charities are not looking ahead they are not prepared to meet changing priorities or future needs. This means charities run the risk of quickly becoming less relevant in a rapidly changing economic and social environment.

It is easy to blame charities for this myopia. But, as Dan Corry points out "Charities are not irrational – they are responding to huge range of different incentives" (Corry 2020). Charity leaders may well wish to take the long view and to develop and respond in a strategic and agile way, but there are a number of barriers they encounter in doing this. Some of these barriers are the result of the explicit regulations that are placed on charities' operations, others are implicit and result from the expectations placed on charities from the outside, as well as the culture within a charity itself.

The Problem of Governance

The Charity Commission regulates the type of cause that can be registered as a public benefit – *what* charities can do – and also sets out very specific rules on how charities are run – *how* they do it. Unlike businesses, charities always have to be overseen by a board of trustees under rules set out in its governing documents (which have to be approved by the Charity Commission). Trustees are almost always volunteers, they are responsible for setting the strategic direction for the charity and, for the minority of charities that employ paid staff, but which we are concerned with here, trustees are expected to leave the operational work to the paid staff. However, in those thousands of charities with no paid staff, the trustees also run the charity. In some charities, trustees are current or former users of the service, with very specific insights and connections into the charity's work on the ground (disability charities and community-based charities tend to lead the way in this).

Trustees may however underestimate the level of responsibility that their role confers. Kids Company trustees (a group of very experienced, very senior people) were held largely responsible for the dramatic failure of that charity and, at the time of writing, and had to challenge (successfully) the Charity Commission's decision to disqualify them from running a company for a limited period (Financial Times 2017). This case, alongside the stories critical of charities run by national newspapers including *The Times, The Daily Mail, The Telegraph* and other national newspapers, have highlighted the increased scrutiny that charities, and therefore their trustees, are under (Hurst 2020, Ainsworth 2018, Penna 2020).

In recent years the Charity Commission has drawn criticism from the charity sector for what many feel has been a heavy-handed approach. Its more interventionist style is a change of direction for the Commission (Whitehead 2020). Andrew Hind describes a very different approach when he ran the regulator (from 2004 to 2010):

> The charity regulator does not exist to limit a charity's options or constrain its actions. Restriction will not assist the growth of the charity sector nor benefit the millions of beneficiaries it helps.
>
> *(Hind 2011)*

However, the Charity Commission today is operating under very different circumstances. At the time of writing, in 2020, the dip in public trust in charities has been widely publicised (Populus and Charity Commission 2018). Where there is less trust, the instinct is to ask a regulator to step in with rules and enforcement. In its annual report the Charity Commission makes it clear that public expectations of charities are different from the expectations placed on other organisations:

> People are united in one fundamental expectation: that a charity is more than an organisation with worthy aims – it should be a living example of charitable purpose, and of the attitudes, and behaviours which the public expect.
>
> *(Charity Commission 2019)*

In other words, the public expects excellence in the *way* that charities do their work, not just in the type of work they do.

It is not therefore enough for a charity to provide additional care to disabled young people, which helps them to live fulfilling lives, if its staff are not paid the living wage, their wellbeing at work is not supported, or if there is a dramatic gender pay gap in the workforce. As Noel Hyndman observes:

> [Charities'] strength comes from the value society places on the social capital that they generate, and the trust and confidence that society has in them and their employees.

Hyndman goes on to warn that, conversely, an inappropriate response by charities, i. e. one which is discordant with public expectations, "can jeopardize their lofty and valuable roles, and undermine focus, value and trust" (Hyndman 2017: 152).

Charities then are not simply neutral vehicles pursuing causes: the way in which they do their work is under more scrutiny than ever before. This is just one example of the creeping expectations in the sector, which place more and more requirements on a charity, and on its governing trustees. This in turn means that charities need to recruit trustees with a very broad range and high level of skills. Smaller local charities, which lack the attractive brands of national charities, may struggle to find people with the skills and the time to join their boards. A lack of skills combined with a low level of turnover on a trustee board can also be damaging to charities, as longstanding chairs and trustees, however talented, can lack the fresh perspective needed to challenge and to move a charity forward. A limited intake of new trustees can lead to gaps in skills, and a poorly functioning board can lead into a circle of decline, by putting off potential new trustees from joining. After all, who wants to give up their evenings to long, dysfunctional board meetings with difficult people?

Trustees wield significant power in a charity, and a chief executive's ability to shape and direct the charity has to be negotiated carefully with their trustees. This means that the power in a charity can, and should be, diffuse. The chief executive of a charity is really the agent of the governing board, and the board needs to ensure that the charity's work is all directed towards achieving its public benefit. This diffuse power structure is not easy to grasp for anyone outside the sector, and it throws up some weird and wonderful challenges for anyone wanting to bring about change within a charity.

Size Matters

When members of the public are asked to think of a charity they tend to think of national charities with a big brand (Populus and Charity Commission 2018). Very few think immediately of small, local charities, and yet the majority of UK charities are more like the tenants organisation I was involved with in Camden: run on a shoestring, housed in 'meanwhile' space awaiting development, where plumbing leaks and vermin infestations were too frequent to get worked up about. The staff in these tiny charities are often dedicated, part-time and underpaid. Huge amounts of work, including knocking on doors and delivering leaflets and surveys, is done by a network of volunteers, all local residents. The trustees are all current or former private tenants with a mix of local knowledge and core skills (communications, fundraising, politics, finance and knocking-heads-together – aka community development). No one has much time or much money.

Amongst the tens of thousands of charities registered with the Charity Commission, there are many small, volunteer-run, community-based groups like the one I describe above. In fact 80% of all charities have no paid staff and 82% run on less than £10,000 per year (NCVO 2019a). But UK charities also include multi-million-pound organisations running complex services and managing significant investments. Some are just enormous, with turnovers of more than £100m per year. These include funders (such as the Wellcome Trust) and almost all are household names such as the National Trust, Citizens Advice or the National Theatre (NCVO 2018). One-third of these so-called *super-major* charities are involved in social care activities (Mencap, NSPCC and St John's Ambulance for example). This can mean that they are delivering essential services to vulnerable people nationwide, they operate with complex management and funding structures, employ trained professionals in every aspect of their services and core team, and need to work closely with statutory services like health, social care or probation.

Charities overall employ around 3% of the UK workforce and, while most of these people work in small organisations with fewer than 50 staff, the super-major charities are also major employers (NCVO 2020): the National Trust, in addition to its huge volunteer workforce, employed more than 8,000 people in January 2021; Save the Children International employed more than 17,500 (Clark 2021). These are charities working in ways which, by their very scale, demand a completely different approach to that of local community-based groups. And the public also has a very different reaction to charities according to their size: asked to rate their perception of charities, people clearly distinguish between large and small with 57% saying they are more likely to trust small charities over large ones (34%) (Populus and Charity Commission 2018).

Paradoxically though, the public is also more inclined to give generously to the large charities than to the smaller ones. And the ways that charities are governed (with some proportionate changes for micro charities) and the expectations around their work remain the same, whatever their size. While charities have evolved to work in new areas on a completely different scale, public opinion hasn't evolved along with them. The public often seems shocked and alarmed at the 'professionalisation' of the sector, and the changes to structure and culture that working at scale brings. For example, 60% of people reported that their trust in charities had diminished due to concerns that charities were spending too much money on 'advertising / wages / admin' (Populus and Charity Commission 2018: 9) and yet, as we shall see, these are essential elements of running a successful organisation and in fact this infrastructure is routinely under-resourced in the charity sector.

Chasing the Money

There is of course enormous variation in the way in which all these different charities generate income to carry out their public benefit. Individual donors like you and me still make up the largest single source of funding for UK charities at 47%, or £25.4bn in 2017/18. The second largest source of funding was government (local and national) which made up 29% of charities' funding in 2017/18 (NCVO 2020).

Although the total amount of funding that charities secure from the state (through local, national government, or NHS trusts, for example) has remained relatively stable, the nature of this funding has altered over the last 15 years. Rather than offering grants to charities, state authorities have moved to offer contracts instead (House of Lords 2017: 41). This shift has triggered a change in the types of charities we find around us. Over the last ten years the mid-sized bracket of charities (£100,000–£1m turnover) has been hollowed out as public grant programmes were cut, and more government money went to larger charities in the form of contracts (NCVO 2020).

Prior to the period of cuts to government expenditure from 2010 onwards, many small charities could apply for grants from their local council or health service. Grants set out specific pieces of work, for a set period of time and had some negotiated (usually light-touch) targets attached. Since 2010 local authorities, under pressure to cut costs, have accelerated their move away from grant funding and towards commissioning for larger contracts and inviting charities, alongside for-profit companies, to apply to deliver services.

Contracting favours much larger charities, as government and health services tend to bundle work into larger contracts, which only organisations above a certain size, turnover and capacity are able to apply for. Applying for, negotiating and delivering contracts also requires specific skills and experience in the charity's core staff which many small to mid-sized charities simply lack and can't afford to buy in. This was not a process designed with a small charity in mind, as research from Lloyd's Bank Foundation has revealed:

> This move towards larger contracts has seen small and medium-sized charities lose up to 44% of their income from public bodies. For the charities providing evidence from 120 tender processes, more than half reported that they were either prevented from bidding or they were unsuccessful. Even those that secured some money reported many difficulties in the process.
>
> *(Lloyds Bank Foundation 2016: 4)*

Even where charities do manage to win statutory contracts these are often a mixed blessing, locking the organisation into contracts that may be at odds with the actual needs of the people the charity aims to support. At worst, contracts can be a financial and resource black hole, as public sector clients (under pressure from politicians and taxpayers) may demand cost savings. This means that charities often 'already struggle to make ends meet' due to the way in which the contract is configured, and then may also find themselves having to meet any additional costs of the contract using the charity's unrestricted funding (Lloyds Bank Foundation 2016: 6).

Paying the Piper

A peculiar aspect of charity funding, and one which holds back a charity's responsiveness, is what President Emerita of the Heron Foundation Clara Miller describes as "the looking glass world of nonprofit money" (Miller 2005): the fact that there is rarely a direct relationship between the funder and the person receiving support. Charities usually operate as intermediaries, devising and delivering the services they judge are needed by groups in society. The people who pay for these services though are not those who use them.

Funders (individual donors, charitable trusts and sections of government and local authorities) pay for the services which a charity says are needed for a particular cause or group of service users. This is very different from the way that a traditional business operates because there is no immediate feedback loop that rewards responsiveness and excellence. Whereas in business, sales (or lack of sales) quickly orientate a for-profit company in the direction of the customer, in charities the service users don't usually have an opportunity to shop around.

A charity's income does not depend on direct feedback to guide the type and quality of services it runs or how it runs them, and there aren't sales and profits to guide decisions for the charity (or the funder). Instead, charities rely largely on trust: funders trust charities' expertise and insight to decide on the most appropriate service for the people they are supposed to be helping, and funders also trust in charities to deliver this service in the best way.

This is one reason why market-forces incentives and commercial operations do not map easily onto charities (although various ways to graft these on have been tried, as we shall see). One of the results of this gap between feedback and delivery has been a lack of competition on the quality of services. Charities do not compete directly for beneficiaries on the quality of their services. This gap has denuded charities of one impetus to innovate, competition, which impels for-profit companies. Another result of this gap is that charities are playing to two different, and potentially conflicting, stakeholders at the same time: their funders and their service users.

Trading One-Handed

With the steady reduction in grant funding since 2010, charities have been under growing pressure to diversify their sources of income. Funders routinely ask charities to demonstrate how they are diversifying their income and how else they will fund themselves 'sustainably' at the end of any proposed funding term. Although funders have always asked for this, over the last decade charity leaders have faced narrowed options and increased competition for the trusts and foundation grants which might have helped them achieve this diversification (Radojev 2018). Charities are encouraged to find new ways of generating income and this has fuelled charities' willingness to embrace commissioned contracts (however uncomfortable), and it is also why many charities now look to trading services and products to raise cash.

Trading, for charities, is nothing new. In one form, the charity shop, it is reassuringly familiar. However, in other forms, such as selling products to the vulnerable people a charity is helping, or hiring out its premises at private-sector prices, a charity's entrepreneurialism may not always sit comfortably with the public's expectations. Indeed, Gina Miller, creator of the short-lived True and Fair Foundation, in her foundation's report *Hornet's Nest* (now no longer available) attempted to make the case that charities should not trade at all (Cass Business School undated.a).

Every so often, the reality of today's charities smashes headfirst into our assumptions about the charity world. In 2016 the Sun reported that Age UK had been overcharging for insurance to older people through a partnership with E.ON. It then emerged that Age UK had made millions of pounds in total through its commercial arm, Age UK Enterprises Ltd (Brignall 2016). A review by Ofgem later concluded that there was no case to open an investigation, but the Charity Commission sensed a disjuncture between the legal obligations of Age UK and public expectations of it as a charity. Age UK conceded that it needed to be more transparent about its trading relationships and activities. Trading presents some interesting challenges to charities, but it also presents a major challenge to public understanding of charities, feeding into some uncertainties about what charities are and what they should be.

Reputation is Everything

As we've seen, charities today are not always easy to categorise. In fact this heterogeneity has been a characteristic of the sector for much of its history, contrary to the myth of a simpler 'golden age' of charities (NCVO 2004). The reality of charities can be at odds with the common idea of a charity: while many charities have adapted successfully to the changing environment they find themselves in, sometimes they may find that public opinion hasn't caught up with the reality of their world and its pressures. This huge range of work, culture and size makes it incredibly challenging to pin down charity in a single definition. Pete Alcock has lumped charities together as a not-very-enticing-sounding 'non-profit residuum' (Alcock 2010). Despite their variety, charities still tend to be seen as belonging to one single homogeneous sector, and are treated largely the same in terms of regulation and public expectations.

The sector as a whole was regarded with particular distaste after a sad event in 2015. In that year a 92-year-old, Olive Cooke, took her own life, and one of the contributing factors (although not the direct reason for her death according to her family) was said to be the large number of heart-rending direct mailshots she received from charities (Morris 2016). Charities which Cooke had donated to were sharing or selling on her data to others, and it was estimated that in the year she died she had received as many as 3,000 fundraising direct mailshots (ibid).

For many, this case revealed a dark side of the charity world. Here was not one, but a large number of well-known charities behaving more like ruthless businesses than much-loved charities. They were selling donor data; they were employing third party (usually commercial) companies to run direct mail campaigns; they were engaging in the sort of hard-hitting marketing appeals that could be harmful to vulnerable people. In fact, they were responsible for exactly the sort of targeted and emotionally exploitative marketing which some charities campaign against, when this marketing is aimed at vulnerable groups and undertaken by for-profit businesses (for example advertising high-sugar foods near to schools).

Suddenly the public was shocked, not only by one elderly woman's death but by the unexpected vision of charities that the story revealed, prompting a sense of unease about the charity sector (Radojev 2016). What did it mean to be a charity when the organisation was prepared to resort to these methods to pursue its cause? Was it really acceptable for a charity to claim that any means justified its ends if those ends were their stated 'public benefit'?

This reaction suggested a disconnect between the charitable cause and methods charities use to pursue their cause, a disconnect which the sector is still working through today. Since 2015 we've seen shockwaves running through the sector on other issues: safeguarding vulnerable people in the developing world, BAME representation in leadership, gender pay gaps, staff wellbeing and bullying. All of these relate to the disconnect between reality and perception. The public expects charities to operate to the highest ethical standards – higher, perhaps much higher, than ordinary businesses. But charities are also expected to be efficient and effective enough to compete with traditional businesses.

Following the Olive Cooke case large charities started apologising for some sharp fundraising practices, they agreed to establish a voluntary code of practice and later largely supported a fundraising regulator. However, the CEOs of smaller charities piped up with an understandable sense of resentment. Smaller charities had not engaged in these kinds of direct marketing fundraising (partly because they could not afford it); they resented the behaviour of these large charities which was tarnishing the name of the sector as a whole. They were also nervous that this behaviour would usher in yet more onerous regulations. This further illustrates the huge challenge of trying to support such a varied sector to grow and develop: the policies and campaigning which could help one set of charities to meet their future challenges might be irrelevant, or even damaging, for others.

Trust

Where this sense of unease prevails in the public imagination, trust can be eroded. As 2018 research by Populus for the Charity Commission showed, people reported that their trust in charities had reduced as a result of negative stories in the media, and due to their perception that charities spend too much money on wages, advertising and administration (an issue we'll return to) (Populus and Charity Commission 2018). Some UK newspapers have been highly critical of charities, the Daily Mail has taken a lead on this with stories clustering around how charities spend their income and charity CEO salaries. In June 2019 one of the charities the Daily Mail wrote about actually took them to court, forcing the newspaper to both pay damages and publish an apology (Weaver 2019), but the negative effect of this long-running campaign has trickled into our national consciousness, as Populus research shows (Populus and Charity Commission 2018: 9).

When charities do not reach the standards expected by the public, trust in the sector as a whole is affected and so are donations, as the charity press frequently reminds me with headlines about the consequences of errant behaviour by charities making an appearance in my inbox. In this environment of intense introspection, combined with a more active regulator, it is understandable that most charities feel defensive and that they focus on battening down the hatches and simply focusing on survival. However, it is that very instinct that, ironically, could ultimately lead charities' decreasing relevance. Focusing on survival, and the defensiveness this breeds, may prevent those inside the sector from looking out at a changing world and spotting the emerging issues where help and resource is needed most.

2

WHAT ARE CHARITIES FOR?

Case Study: Church Mission Society

When Ali Bateman arrived at Church Mission Society (CMS) as its new CEO the organisation was already 219 years old. This charity was started by a group of social reformers in 1799. Members of the Clapham Sect had campaigned for the end of the slave trade and social reform in industrial Britain and they were also committed to evangelism. They set up CMS to send missionaries around the world to 'make the gospel of Jesus known and understood' and they sent them to a truly astounding list of countries over the years. Their legacy is still visible today, notably in Anglican churches around the world, in education and in healthcare initiatives. But the charity's founding was bound up in the history of empire, which struck a discordant note as the decades wore on. CMS had adapted its work over the years, shifting its emphasis from sending out British missionaries to the furthest corners of the globe, to funding local partners to deliver projects around the world. As incoming CEO, Bateman was intent on asking himself, members, trustees and staff some searching questions:

1. If CMS had been working on its mission for 200 years and had not achieved its aims yet, had it failed?
2. Was its work really making a difference? How could it be more effective?
3. Were there new routes the charity could go down to re-imagine its mission in the 21st century?

In order to do this the charity went through what they describe as a 're-founding process:' returning to the founding story and experience of CMS, connecting with the energy of that time and then creatively applying that to today's most urgent needs.

For the charity, and its many, longstanding and highly committed supporters these questions were challenging to consider. But Bateman saw his arrival as an

DOI: 10.4324/9781003139089-2

opportunity to re-appraise and re-examine assumptions. He wanted to see whether CMS could in future reach outside its existing audiences and embrace new ideas and actions (Bateman 2020).

When we start to consider how charities can and should evolve to tackle the issues of the future it is important to understand the role they play in society. This might seem obvious on the face of it, but the more that researchers dig into this, the less clear the answer is to the question: what are charities for? Tackling the causes which the state will not and/or cannot reach, responding quickly to emerging needs where the state and the private sector just wouldn't mobilise, this is what we imagine charities are for. Charities are supposed to be responsive, to fill in the gaps, large and small, between the state and the private sector.

The valued and distinctive features of the UK charity sector are articulated by charity workers themselves as:

> being able to question and voice the concerns of its communities, to champion unpopular causes, to cater for the needs of 'outliers', reaching those parts of society others can't, or won't, reach and addressing 'wicked issues'.
>
> *(Alcock, Butt & Macmillan 2013)*

But do charities *really* address wicked problems and champion unpopular causes? Is the way that charities are set up really designed for them to bridge these 'outlier' gaps between the state and the private sector, and respond where there is most need?

If we do believe that some charities exist to address wicked and outlier issues, we might expect them to be focused on the gaps and needs in society today. However, as we shall see, the existing data is poor on this, and that data, which does exist, does not appear to show that charities are tackling areas of most urgent concern to society.

Charities are required to deliver a public benefit, as we have seen, but no one sets out which public benefits our society is most in need of at any time, or where (Dundee? Neath? Great Yarmouth?) these needs are most acute. Instead, the philosophy around the registration of new charities, in which the Charity Commission must register any organisation which meets the requirements of a charity, is to let a thousand flowers bloom. This creative anarchy has great potential. By allowing for the birth of multiple, overlapping, new charities we may allow for the emergence of disruptive new services and ideas that have the freedom to respond to emerging issues and to tackle them in new and exciting ways.

But this creativity depends on a category of people we know relatively little about: charity founders. Can we expect founders to know enough to start charities on the issues that really matter, in the places where they are needed most? Charities emerge, and either succeed or fail, in an organic way. They are founded on the inspiration of one individual, or a group of people, with a passion for a cause. This passion is needed to get a charity off the ground, but it doesn't always mean that the charities we get reflect the most pressing issues in society.

One former charity CEO I interviewed for this book identified two divergent views of the role of charities and these contrasting views recurred throughout my discussions of this question:

> It depends whether you think our role is to smooth things over, to offer a sticking plaster, or to change the world. I don't know about you but I gave up a lot to work in this sector, and it wasn't to administer a sticking plaster!
>
> *(Interviewee S)*

When I talk to anyone who has ambitions to enter the charity sector, this expectation of being able to effect change is an important motivator. But it is not the only reason that charities exist, these reasons are complex and varied. This variation stems from the peculiar historical origins of charities, and the impact that these origins have on the structure and psychology of the sector is wide-reaching even today.

Anyone can start a charity and its work can cover any one of the very long list of causes set out in the Charity Act 2011. Although the Act has tried to pin down the purpose of charities in law, the work that charities undertake remains broad. It ranges from delivering services that used to be the domain of local authorities, to large-scale disaster relief, to conservation, heritage, health and campaigning for changes to the law. While charities have a purpose that is written on paper and lodged with the Charity Commission, they can also have important undeclared missions. These are unwritten, cultural and emotional, they may even be subconscious, and they stem from the charity's people, its origins and its history. In particular this underlying culture is shaped by the charity's founder and its subsequent leadership.

The Origin Story

The idea of charity is ancient and is intertwined with religion. Much has been written about whether there is a human instinct to behave altruistically and the connection this has to the modern charity. Early British charities were intimately connected to churches, tithes and alms-giving (Jordan 2016). They functioned in a world with no welfare state and, though many were consumed with religious matters, where the state did not exist to provide education, medical care or alms to the poor, individual philanthropists or the church sometimes stepped in to fill the gaps (Bubb 2017).

Evidence of this early charity can still be seen today in many of our towns and cities. In the small town where I grew up the beautiful art nouveau library was endowed by the Scottish-American philanthropist Andrew Carnegie in 1906. But philanthropists like Carnegie had their own agenda: Carnegie wanted to help the 'deserving poor', a distinction first made in the 1834 Poor Law and which has shadowed welfare policy ever since (Golightly and Holloway 2016). Carnegie's deserving poor were:

(the) industrious and ambitious; not those who need everything done for
them, but those who, being most anxious and able to help themselves,
deserve and will be benefited by help from others.

(Carnegie 1889: 686)

His name is still emblazoned across the library entrance, though this act of philanthropy belies the ruthlessness with which he ran his business interests, including the brutal putting-down of the 1892 Homestead Strike.

In London many of the hospitals we know well today were originally charitable foundations, as were schools such as Eton College, which was originally
founded in 1440 by Henry VII to provide education for 70 poor boys (Eton
2020).[1] In post-industrial revolution England, the extreme urban poverty shocked
some people into philanthropic action. Some philanthropists were wealthy tra-
vellers. American philanthropist George Peabody was shocked by the appalling
squalor of London's housing in the late 1800s and he funded some of the first
social housing in Spitalfields – again ringfenced for the 'deserving poor' with strict
and enforced regulations on work and behaviour – in a venture that eventually
developed into the Peabody housing association we know today.

Filling in the Gaps Today

If early philanthropy developed to fill gaps and meet needs, it only succeeded in
doing so in an incomplete way. Following the social and economic disruption of the
two world wars in the twentieth century it became clear that charities alone were
unable to provide the scale and consistency of support needed across society.[2] In
1942 the UK government adopted the Beveridge Report and committed to providing universal basic support for those most in need, while recognising that charities
still had an important role to play. As a result, today's charities operate in a very different world. In the UK we have a National Health Service and a social security
system which offer a safety net (albeit reduced in recent years) for those in greatest
need. There are still gaps where the state cannot or will not step in. These gaps lie in
the development of new and nimble responses to emerging issues, where for example state-led support can take many years to set up; or in non-urgent but vital pre-
ventative work. There may also be gaps in instances where state provision is felt to be
inadequate and where charities develop a more effective intervention.

In society today we face existing and emerging issues to which the government
(local and national) is struggling to respond, and where private business lacks the
incentives to do so. Scenario planning work has identified the emerging trends likely
to shape our world to 2045 as being: demographic changes (including ageing,
migration and urbanisation); increased individualism (an expectation of individual
empowerment and greater diffusion of power); likely increased demand for food,
power and water; the impact of new technology, and an increased likelihood of
global natural disasters (Cordery, Smith and Berger 2017). At the time of writing the

global Covid-19 pandemic has highlighted vulnerability to infectious diseases and raised awareness of significant global and regional inequalities.

These are challenges which charities should, theoretically, be uniquely well placed to tackle, for example by exploring and refining responses that could then be scaled up. However, Charity Commission data on the number of charities working on particular causes does not seem to show that these major and emerging causes are reflected in the make-up of the sector. This could be because of the quality of the data available, in which the areas of public benefit are so wide as to be uninformative. For example innovative grant-makers such as Llankelly Chase may seem simply like a small-scale funder in the Commission's statistics, whereas in fact this small foundation is developing some radical and far-reaching systems-change work. Similarly the charities listed under 'environmental' could range from campaigning organisations tackling climate change to local conservation trusts challenging building developments.

Published figures on charities are highly generalised, lumping together charities of very different sizes, services and scope. However, they do provide a snapshot of the areas on which charitable work is focused. Those causes which appear in the greatest number are, in bald terms, those that motivated the most people to found their own charity. As charities stay registered for many years, whether or not they are still very active, it is perhaps most helpful to look at the registration of new charities for an indication of which causes inspire the highest number of people to found new charities.

From these headline figures it appears that the cause that inspired by far the greatest number of people to found charities in 2016–18 was that of 'culture and recreation'. It seems on the face of it that this category does not reflect the areas of greatest social and environmental need, although the breadth of this data category makes it difficult to assess this with any certainty (Figure 2.1).

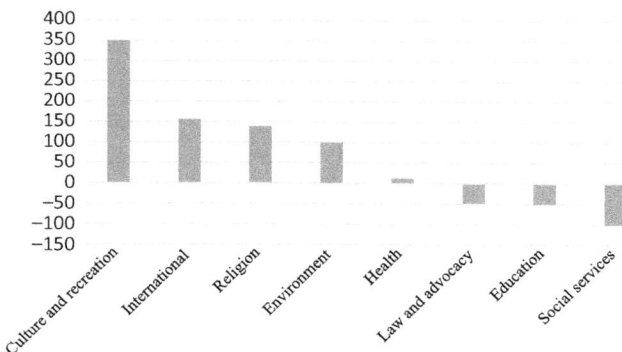

FIGURE 2.1 Net increase and decrease in number of registered charities by cause between 2016–2018

Source: NCVO (2019a, 2020). This excludes research and grant-making.

Working in the Places With Greatest Need?

Charities are not evenly distributed across the UK. While we might expect charities to be concentrated in the geographical areas of greatest need, reflecting a responsiveness to social and environment issues at a local level, research has shown that the opposite may be true. The reported geographical concentration of charities doesn't appear to reflect the areas that most need their support. In 2020 New Philanthropy Capital (NPC) reported that the wealthier areas of the country enjoy an above-average number of charities on their doorstep, providing a wide range of services. By contrast some of the poorest towns, which are ranked as high on the Indices of Multiple Deprivation, have fewer than the average number of charities. Blackpool, number one on the 2019 Indices has only 0.6 charities per 1,000 people, compared with the regional average of 1.4 and the national average of 1.8. More affluent areas had many more charities: for example the Cotswolds (272 on the Indices) had 5.5 charities per 1,000 (Corry 2020a: 2).

These figures seem to indicate that a kind of reverse osmosis seems to be underway, in which charitable resources (volunteers, founders and donations, i.e. 'social activity') are being generated in areas that are less deprived. However, it is important to treat these figures with caution, as the NPC itself notes, the data is incomplete and this research aimed to encourage further research. The location at which a charity is registered only provides part of the picture, as many larger charities will be registered at their London headquarters, for example, but operate in many other parts of the UK. Similarly, the location of some of the most deprived wards in the country within some of our wealthiest regions should not be overlooked.

However a pattern of seeing a concentration of 'social activity' in wealthier areas, and relatively less activity in poorer areas, was also evident in the flurry of volunteering activity related to Covid-19 in early 2020. In news stories about the first wave of the pandemic the community response, through 'mutual aid' groups, was lauded. The New Local Government Network reported on the way these groups were established and run, providing a useful early insight into the achievements of, and challenges faced by, these organisations. This report makes clear that areas with high existing social capital were much more likely to develop functioning and effective mutual aid groups. Conversely, disadvantaged areas with lower existing numbers of charities and volunteers (precisely the areas where Covid-19 incidence mapping later showed there were the greatest levels of infections and deaths) were less likely to benefit from mutual aid (with the caveat that volunteer support may happen in a less formal way) (Tiratelli and Kaye 2020).

Founder Foundations – Inspiration or Whim?

Charity founders are often lauded for their work, indeed a well-connected few find their way into every list of New Year and Birthday honours, and founders are widely respected for what they do. They are, after all, volunteers who give up their time, and often their own money, to set up charities to tackle a cause that really matters to them. It is usual to project altruistic motivations on charity founders, but do charity founders take a dispassionate view of the world around them and identify problems which need solving, or issues to be tackled? Do they examine the evidence of need and take account of any other existing provision, before going on to develop the most effective means of filling that gap?

The answer is … no one knows. There is very little research into charity founders, but it would be extremely interesting to see an exploration of the motivations and characteristics of this group. It would be fascinating to know whether there are significant commonalities in their backgrounds, personalities and motivations. Nevertheless, the fact is that it is not necessary for founders to set up a charity on an objective examination of the facts, or of need. Founders are not required to demonstrate that their new charity will *not* be duplicating the work of another. They are not required to demonstrate that there is a demand for their proposed work.

In one of very few studies touching on the question of charity founders (albeit related to the US non-profit sector), Susan Rose-Ackerman hypothesised that people may be more likely to found charities if they are 'ideologues' (i.e. if "they have strong beliefs about the proper way to provide a particular service"). As ideologues they may be attracted by a combination of avoiding the influence of external investors, and the comparative tax advantages of the charity status (Rose-Ackerman 1996: 719)

This implies that founders are highly motivated and driven, and that they are likely to have a significant passion for their chosen cause. The founders of some of today's larger UK charities were motivated by an emotional response to a situation, for example both Shelter and Crisis, now two major UK homelessness charities, were both founded in response to the powerful 1960s film, *Cathy Come Home*, which brought to life the impact of homelessness on a family. The fact that charities may be founded as a result of an individualistic or subjective response does not mean that these charities do not do valuable work, or that they aren't meeting a real need. But it is interesting to observe that charity founders are likely, at least in part, to act on a highly personal, emotional response to problems they perceive in society.

This is important because it points up an interesting contradiction. When charities speak about their work and their mission they refer exclusively to public benefit, but the very foundation of each charity, emanating as it does from the action of a private individual, implies a private benefit also. It isn't unreasonable to conjecture that in starting a charity a founder does, in addition to creating a public benefit, also derive some personal benefit, whether that is an outlet for grief, a sense of agency or value, perhaps even a boost to the ego.

This hints at a division at the centre of the charity's purpose, implying that charities are not just for the benefit of their service users but also bring a benefit to the founder, to trustees, to volunteers and to staff (an aspect we will explore further later in this book). This is significant because it offers an insight into why it may be difficult for charities to adopt an entrepreneurial approach to their work, to ditch projects with poor outcomes and develop fresh services, and to think ahead to what the big new emerging issues are and how they will respond to them. If charities do in some way retain an ethos of being led by an emotional response to circumstances, then calls on them to be data-driven, to measure impact or to demonstrate efficiency, feel like an imposition, and counter to their culture. As charities grow larger, and are pushed to adopt more of these 'professionalised' ways of working, we might expect some of these tensions to come to the fore.

Of course, some charities are founded in response to objective evidence of significant issues in society. But, while this more evidence-driven charity creation can happen, it is not required. There is nothing to stop someone setting up a new charity duplicating or potentially even undermining the work of other existing charities. The most obvious examples of this are charities set up in response to a bereavement. There are countless tiny cancer charities set up by bereaved families, the latest to catch my attention being the Ruth Strauss foundation, set up by cricketer Sir Andrew Strauss. No doubt Strauss had the best of intentions in setting up a new charity, and he was in the enviable position of being able to garner some incredible free advertising during the 2020 test series against the West Indies, which almost automatically resulted in more than £878,000 of donations (Sky Sports 2020). There are, however, thousands of cancer charities in the UK, and the match featuring the Ruth Strauss Foundation took place in the same week that Cancer Research UK announced enormous cuts to its workforce and its research work as a result of a loss of fundraising due to Covid-19 (Cooney 2020).

I think it is reasonable to ask whether Andrew Strauss's efforts could have been even more effective had he chosen to support one of the existing major cancer charities (which already has its own board, its own CEO and back office) or to have set up an administratively less onerous donor advised fund (DAF). When he set up his foundation he would have been under no obligation to make a business case to the Charity Commission for this new charity and to demonstrate how it added something to the myriad cancer charities already in existence. Of course he is perfectly entitled to set up a charity for emotional reasons, but some have argued that in the charity sector there are 'too many entrances and not enough exits' (Corry 2014). There is in fact no ideal number of charities to be registered but it is worth noting that there are relatively few barriers to anyone wanting to set up a new charity, with 79% of applicants successful (National Audit Office 2013: 25) and new registrations outnumbering charities removed by an average of 10% (Burne James 2015). There are limited incentives to close down charities once they are registered and there is no one (except donors) to stop charities running services that are ineffective (or to assess effectiveness).

Does Funding Follow Need?

Charities aren't necessarily set up to respond to an evidenced need, but the types of service-delivery and campaigning charities that we are primarily concerned with in this book will usually need to demonstrate that they are responding to a need in society in order to attract funding. Without appeal to funders (individual donors, government or trusts), non-endowed charities cannot survive for long, so perhaps we could look to funders – rather than founders – to push charities to be responsive to the emerging issues for our society? After all, funders will determine which charities thrive and they may exercise a corrective function by rewarding the most relevant charities. Can we rely on funders to ensure that existing charities tackle the issues that matter most? Can the focus of available funding inspire the set-up or re-orientation of charities towards the causes where there is most emerging need?

In my first charity job I brought together workers running hostels and projects for homeless people in various charities across London. One of the most impressive projects I visited was in south London and it supported female sex workers to manage and then overcome their addictions and to practise safe sex (Shelter 2004: 13–15). It didn't require them to stop working before they could get accommodation, it also didn't insist that the beneficiaries were sober before they were housed and supported. At that time women with such complex needs would usually be evicted from hostels very quickly (those hostels they were allowed into in the first place), but this project saw only 17% evictions in its first year. Female sex workers are a vulnerable group for whom few support services existed. There was clearly a need for this work and this seemed to me a powerful example of where a charity could offer something which the state and the private sector simply could not: no private company would ever make a profit from a project like this, and the state – good at large-scale interventions – would struggle to provide the individualised support needed by this group of women, who were also highly suspicious of anything that smacked of officialdom.

This was one example of exactly the sort of work we think the charity sector does well: an outlier project reaching people whom other services may not be able to. But for the charity running it, the project presented a paradox: the charity was meeting a clear need, but getting donations to support projects on unpopular causes like this is an uphill struggle. While some trusts and foundations recognise the need for projects like this (Lloyd's Bank Foundation is an excellent example) individual donors and corporate donors may blanch at the prospect of supporting this kind of work.

While individual donors still make up the largest source of charity funding, donors do not give money to charity based on an objective appraisal of the most important issues, alongside some analysis of the most effective types of project to tackle each issue. Recent attention given to the 'effective altruism' movement has brought this issue to the fore. Effective altruism is the targeted investment of philanthropic money in the causes which are the most likely to affect change (MacAskill 2015). Taking into account the areas of greatest need and the requirement for robust evidence, in its purest form this is likely to focus on international aid and health inequalities. While the model is compelling in theory, it risks missing the fundamental founding element of philanthropy by ignoring the emotional basis on which these giving decisions are made. As we have long understood in the disciplines of marketing and politics, decisions aren't influenced by facts as much as emotion. Decisions to donate will, in a similar way, be determined by a donor's emotional response.

CAF's annual report on giving trends sheds some light on individual donation decisions. There are two ways of exploring which causes are most important to donors in the UK. One is to review by the frequency with which donations are made to a cause another is to look at the total amount each cause receives from individual donors. Both measures are quite crude, and easily skewed by a few one-off major donations, but they are the best we have.

The top four causes which people reported giving to in 2018 were animal charities (26%), children/young people's charities (26%), medical research (25%) and hospices/hospitals (20%) (CAF 2019: 12). These were unchanged on the previous two years. The causes which received the largest amounts of recent donations however, were rather different. Religious causes received the highest proportion of the total donations (19%) followed by disaster relief (several major international relief operations occurred in 2018), then medical research, young people and animal welfare/hospices (tied at 8%) (CAF 2019: 14). Visibility and personal connection seem to be the salient factors in these giving decisions. People seem to be more willing to give to a charity that is front of mind, perhaps through a bereavement or illness, or from an awareness of one's own vulnerabilities to major illnesses. This is supported by research on major donors in the UK which indicates that donors choose causes that relate to their own life experiences and which support people with whom they feel an affinity (Breeze 2013). This orients giving towards those causes identified by CAF.

Of these causes which resonate most, it is the most visible brands which secure the highest levels of donations. In 2017, Cats Protection received £31m in bequests while Battersea Cats and Dogs Home received £14.7m. In line with the Matthew Effect[3] of accumulating advantage, the charities that are already financially successful are the charities that can afford to run expensive advertising campaigns to grab our attention and to deliver direct mail marketing campaigns to our doorsteps. It is small wonder then that the wealthiest charities in the country enjoy an entrenched position. As Peter Grant told me, the list of top-30 charities has been little changed for 30 years (Grant 2020). So individual donors are not incentivising charities to tackle the most pressing problems or to support unpopular causes because these are not the issues that donors themselves are emotionally engaged with.

Solving Problems or Softening Impact?

Having explored the reasons why charities are set up and the causes that are more or less likely to attract funding, we should examine the sort of work that charities do in relation to their cause. This returns us to the divergent aims identified for charities at the start of this chapter. Whether they are working on animal welfare or climate change, do charities exist in order to eradicate the problem ('change the world') or to mitigate its impact (apply the 'sticking plaster')?

Many charity CEOs have told me that, in their view, charities' role was ultimately to put themselves out of business, a sentiment which echoes that of the economist Alfred Marshall:

I regard poverty as a passing evil in the progress of man; and I should not like any [poverty relieving] institution started which did not contain in itself the causes which would make it shrivel up, as the causes of poverty itself shrivelled up.

(Dees 2012: 8)

This ultimate aim is reflected in some very ambitious charity mission statements, as we'll see below. But the timescales attached to these missions are often somewhat hazy and I have come across few examples of charities that have actually fulfilled their mission and closed down. Sonia Sodha cites the brave example of MAC UK's founder, Charlie Howard, who set a specific ten-year timescale to their work to change systems around mental health for young people. However, at the time of writing (in 2020) the charity still appears to be going strong after 12 years… (Sodha 2016).

When disaster strikes we expect charities to step in. We see this most often with international aid charities responding to earthquakes and famines, but we also see it closer to home. Following the Grenfell Tower tragedy in 2016 local charities responded immediately to provide shelter and support for residents, reacting with energy and creativity alongside the larger relief charities such as Red Cross. These local charities collaborated with statutory services and managed the overwhelming flow of donations arriving in north Kensington (Muslim Aid 2018). Day-to-day, though, many of these charities ran less well-known services across the wards in north Kensington, services that had grown up around the needs and preferences of the local communities. They ran, and still do run, employment training courses for communities with disproportionately high levels of unemployment. They seek to improve the health of residents with diabetes support sessions, with healthy cooking classes and with community fitness sessions. They bring members of communities together by running cultural projects, and they try to tackle childhood poverty through children's clubs, foodbanks and family support.

These sorts of services represent the life of the typical local charity. They also make up a lot of the project-based services run by larger charities, from return-to-work schemes run by the national Stroke Association to the tenancy sustainment support work run by Crisis, where case workers support formerly homeless people to manage their own tenancies. These are all examples of charities responding to the world around them and trying to make life better for the people they work with. And the quality of these interventions, their aims and their actual impacts vary enormously.

Not all charities though want to work with the world as it is. Some well-known charities set their sights instead (or as well) on tackling the root cause of the problem itself. Crisis, for example, is unequivocal in its ambition to end homelessness. The charity states in 2021, more than 50 years after it was founded, that:

In 21st century Britain, everybody should have a place to live. We need to get Everybody In to end homelessness.

(Crisis 2021).

Stonewall was founded as a campaigning group and it retains an explicitly campaigning mission in 2020:

> We're here to let all lesbian, gay, bi and trans people, here and abroad, know they're not alone. We believe we're stronger united, so we partner with organisations that help us create real change for the better.
>
> *(Stonewall 2021)*

Similarly The Equality Trust, born from a book and then a campaign to reduce inequality states its mission in 2020 as "to improve the quality of life in the UK by reducing socio-economic inequality" (Equality Trust 2021).

Charities may state that they exist to campaign for change, but the largest charities are in fact hybrid organisations, running services that support people to deal with the problem they are seeking to solve, at the same time that they campaign for the problem to be eradicated completely. Housing charity Shelter is a good example of this model: it actively helps people nationwide through its phoneline and housing advice services, and it draws on its case work to make its campaigning work more powerful. Its mission states its hybrid nature particularly clearly at the time of writing:

> Shelter helps millions of people every year struggling with bad housing or homelessness through our advice, support and legal services. And we campaign to make sure that, one day, no one will have to turn to us for help.
>
> *(Shelter 2021)*

Campaigning for change is an obvious role for charities to fulfil, as it is an area which simply could not be fulfilled by the private sector or the public sector. Charities' campaigns themselves are often aimed at one of these actors, to try to change legislation or practice, and the commitment to a mission (the public benefit) rather than achieving a profit should make a non-profit organisation ideally suited to this work. 38 Degrees exists purely to campaign, drawing together online communities around a common cause. Extinction Rebellion created a phenomenal movement to raise awareness about the climate emergency within 12 months. Generation Rent harnessed private renters' sense of injustice and made politicians take notice.

It makes common sense for charities to campaign to tackle problems at their root, but none of these three headline-grabbing examples above is actually a charity. This is because of the restrictions placed on charities around 'political' campaigning, and the more recent challenge of the Lobbying Act.[4] The arrival of the Act increased the sense of jeopardy for charities, in particular smaller ones, of engaging in campaigning. Charities are nervous of falling foul of the legislation, and legal advice to ensure compliance is costly for small charities on a tight budget. The result has been a creeping concern that the sector is being muzzled, as evidenced by the Sheila McKechnie Foundation which found that:

many (charities) are now less inclined to tackle politically challenging issues publicly. Doing so risks meeting both the 'purpose test' and 'public test' of the Act, which requires registration with the Electoral Commission. This is costly, whether organisations register or, instead, try to tread the non-registration side of the line. As a result, those who wish to avoid uncertainty and extra cost are forced to step a very long way back from any potentially challengeable activity

(Sheila McKechnie Foundation 2017: 3)

More pressure has been placed on charities recently by the statements made by the Charity Commission warning charities against getting involved in 'culture wars' and 'political campaigning'. A statement which drew criticism from across the charity sector including from the NCVO (Brindle 2020).

A Need to Adapt

To remain relevant and true to their defining mission charities need to constantly adapt to the changing environment around them. Simply existing for the right motivations (to 'do good', or 'make a difference') is not enough, after all "good motives do not guarantee good outcomes" (Corry 2014). Instead charities have a duty to ensure that they are doing the best possible work to achieve their mission, and this will change and evolve as the world changes around them.

If a charity does not wish to adapt in order to support its service users of the future in the new ways that those people want and need, then it should shut its doors and wind down, having accomplished its mission as it perceives it. The Charity Commission provides a gentle nudge in this direction in their guidance, reminding trustees that they should do what will "best enable the charity to carry out its purposes, both now and for the future". They specifically state that trustees should not be focused on serving the interests of staff or trustees, or preserving the charity "for its own sake" and they explicitly encourage trustees to "consider collaborating or merging with another charity, or even spending all of the charity's resources and bringing it to a close" (Charity Commission 2018:17).

But how many charities are raising their heads above the workload of today to think about the issues of tomorrow, let alone whether they still need to exist? Sometimes a new CEO can bring an opportunity for this disruption and innovation, like Ali Bateman, of Church Mission Society. Bateman spoke to me of the need to lock outside and to challenge practice in the sector: "We are in the bubble of the charity sector [and] should look to who's on the edge, seek new views" (Bateman 2020).

Challenging assumptions about how charities' work maps onto their mission like this is a vital discipline in the sector. One of the fascinating aspects of the Covid-19 situation has been the way it has forced charities to adapt at pace, as thousands of charities have quickly transformed their operations to deal with the crisis. But there is a difference between being able to respond rapidly in a crisis, and thoughtfully planning how a charity will still be able to deliver its mission (or not) in the coming years, as Bateman describes doing at the CMS. Whether we believe that the reason charities exist is to solve problems and to change society for the better, or to mitigate the impacts of major social issues, we need a charity sector that is able to adapt to the changing world around it. But changes to what charities do and how they do it are hard to achieve. Charity services are extremely sticky – even where services are not working, changing them into something more impactful can be an uphill struggle.

Disruption vs. Ossification

Too often in charities I have come across services that were once considered great, even ground-breaking, but which have turned to stone after many years of delivery. One of the most obvious examples of this could be the Kids Company model of intervention. A therapeutic-style 'extended family support' for young people may have worked well on a small scale, but most of the evidence of its effectiveness resided in individual case studies and testimonies. When scaled up across several cities and operating out of multiple centres the effectiveness of interventions does not appear to have been tracked and iterated, with a result that the charity found it difficult to either objectively demonstrate its impact or to improve its services.

Other examples of obsolete charity services that I've regularly seen include advice services which required attendance in person between the hours of 10am to 4pm. While these might have been suitable for people in previous years for who lived locally and did not work, by the 2010s such services excluded the vast number of people balancing mulitple jobs and receiving a complex array of in-work benefits. Similarly, I have come across support groups which, once-active and popular, then ossify, as they remained modelled around existing, ageing, service users and failed to attract newer (younger) members. As a result of a failure to adapt, these services felt exclusive, and attendance dwindled over time. In these examples it is as if Sony, having successfully delivered their original Walkman in 1979, continued to sell the same model in 2020 ignoring the technological changes around them. Charity services, like consumer products, need to adapt, but without the push of direct consumer demand or competition on the quality of services, this adaptation in the charity sector can be sluggish.

Charities are also influenced by unwritten cultural norms, which can hamper innovation. Challenging these assumptions in the organisation can be enough to have a liberating effect and the example of the relationship charity Talk Listen Change (TLC) sets out some of the factors attending a successful charity transformation.

CASE STUDY: TALK LISTEN CHANGE (TLC)

When CEO Michelle Hill joined TLC in 2013 it was an affiliated branch of Relate in Manchester offering integrated relationship support. The charity was an established part of the local voluntary sector, but its model, on which it had run for many years, no longer seemed to be working. When local government cuts hit in the 2010s the charity didn't alter it services or cost base in response, the federated structure with Relate didn't stack up financially and the organisation had been running deficit budgets which were not sustainable. When the CEO of 25 years left the charity the trustees recognised a need for change and Hill, a first time CEO, came in with a mandate to do things differently.

Pivotal to this change was a deep investigation by CEO, staff and trustees into what they stood for as a charity. This allowed them to focus on the outcome they wanted to achieve but freed up their choices around what they would do to achieve this. Going through this process helped them to see clearly that the federated relationship with Relate just wasn't working; it restricted their autonomy and contracts. The Chair of the board was crucial in enabling this change, bringing his business knowledge to bear and supporting Hill's quest to get to a balanced budget and eventually a surplus. While the first year, especially the move away from Relate, was challenging, the charity actually moved to a break even position more speedily than expected and now TLC is a quite different charity. From a turnover of more than £1m in 2013, in 2020 it was budgeting for a £3m turnover and was an important regional player, reaching and supporting people across Greater Manchester. For Hill though there is a recognition that her job is far from finished. She knows that there is always more to be done and charities like TLC have to keep adapting to the changing external environment.

(Hill 2020)

For many charity leaders, a fundamental re-imagining of their work like this can seem overwhelming. Even where they recognise existing services could be better, the difficulties of instigating change are ominous and the drivers for change are often too weak. At TLC Hill had a strong impetus in the form of a burning platform (the deficit), which enabled her to press for radical change, she was also fortunate in having a supportive and able Chair and trustees, and a great deal of staff support also. But in other charities trustees can be averse of change because they are tied emotionally to the existing services, or because they are unable to manage the potential risk of change.

A different culture prevails in the charity world from the business sector. At its most positive it is a culture that motivates staff to achieve a common goal when salaries and working conditions are not great. But a less helpful aspect of charity culture can be its insularity, its tendency to defend existing services against change and to be wary of change. This culture can stem from a fear from charity employees about the unknown and a weariness born of years of enforced (cost-saving) change to services as a result of funding cuts. It can also percolate down from the charity's board, who may feel strong emotional attachment to business-as-usual, even where it isn't very effective. Academic Kimberley Scharf describes this neatly is the 'warm glow' that allows inefficient charities to continue:

'Warm-glow' charities refer to inefficient organisations who carry on operating because they believe their provision is better than other charities raising funds in the same area. They get a warm glow from the work they are doing, regardless of the fact that they are not providing a good service.

(Scharf 2014)

This problem of inertia is sometimes described as the Shirky Principle. This states that complex solutions, like an organisation, company, or an industry, can become so dedicated to the problem they are trying to solve, that they can inadvertently perpetuate the problem.

Charities aren't alone in acting out the Shirky Principle, but perhaps they are particularly at fault when they do so, as the mission at their very heart should be to tackle these problems and they certainly shouldn't end up perpetuating them. This does not imply that charities do this out of a conscious desire to preserve the status quo, it is simply recognising that charities' size and turnover, and their incentives for growth may be such that sustaining the status quo can become their reflex action (Sodha 2016: 21). This principle sheds some light on the way that existing, established charities may struggle to re-orientate themselves towards their core mission and how to interpret it in a rapidly changing world.

Charities which aim to tackle emerging social and environmental issues have a real opportunity to show leadership today, where engaging with, speaking up for and providing support for the communities most affected will be desperately needed. Charities' immense value lies in their being able to "champion unpopular causes", "voice the concerns of its communities", to reach "those parts of society others can't" and address "wicked issues" (Alcock, Butt and Macmillan 2013). But achieving this impact requires some different thinking. It requires charities, funders and trustees to be clear and honest about what each charity is set up to do: whether they are there to tackle problems at root or to deal with the fall-out from issues that others are best placed to tackle; whether the charity founders and funders are motivated only to express their own emotional commitment to a cause, or whether they can expand and build this into a genuine public benefit, even where this means ceding control and adapting their work. It relies on potential founders responding to the issues where there is the greatest need, and it relies on all of us deciding to donate our money to the causes that have the greatest impact for society as a whole.

Notes

1 Today Eton is an expensive and highly selective private school, albeit with some scholarships and bursaries available for exceptional students with a good grounding in the classics and from households unable to afford the £40,000-plus per year fees.
2 While the Royal Commission on Poor Laws and Relief of Distress 2015–9 insisted in its Majority Report that the Poor Laws and their system of locally accountable and funded provision to support the most disadvantaged should remain, the Commission's Minority Report signalled the future path towards a welfare state. The Commission's Minority

Report recognised that the existing system, which relied on local and inconsistent provision was ineffective. The truth of this would be thrown into sharp relief by the social and economic shocks of the First and Second World Wars.

3 Coined by Robert K. Merton in 1968 and derived from the Gospels 'For to everyone who has will more be given, and he will have abundance; but from him who has not, even what he has will be taken away'. *Matthew 25:29.*

4 The Transparency of Lobbying, Non-Party Campaigning and Trade Union Administration Act 2014 (commonly called 'the Lobbying Act').

3

DO CHARITIES REALLY MAKE A DIFFERENCE?

Charities' objectives are diverse, as we have seen, and so our understanding of whether or not a charity is making an impact needs to be tailored to the very specific difference they want to make, and their individual mission. In this chapter we will explore why demonstrating the difference that charities make is so important to their development and future. We will also uncover some of the overt and covert drivers that might prompt charities to undertake this work, and explore just how strong (or weak) these drivers are.

CASE STUDY: CRISIS

At the homelessness charity Crisis it is the board of trustees that hold the charity to account and ensures that it stays true to its values, including 'fearlessness through independence'. Crisis is unusual in that a significant proportion of its funding comes from a large number of individual donors rather than a smaller number of large funders or commissioners. At the start of each year the charity has usually only secured a small proportion of its total budget of around £60m. A situation which Jon Sparkes, its CEO, says leaves them with a combination of the confidence that comes from knowing that the public cares about ending homelessness, and the nervousness that comes from knowing that everything depends on the ability of the charity to raise the necessary funds to achieve this aim.

Being funded by so many individual donors means that no one single funder holds significant sway over the work of Crisis. This unrestricted income gives them unusual freedom in how they spend their money and enormous freedom to be responsive and find creative ways to achieve their mission. However, Sparkes and his board recognise that the downside of individual donor fundraising can be a lack

---

DOI: 10.4324/9781003139089-3

of externally scrutinised governance and standards. Good impact measurement by funders and commissioners can help charities focus on the biggest issues and the most impactful projects, through targets, measurement and regulatory frameworks. Without this sort of external accountability Crisis works hard to evaluate its impact and to ensure a very clear governance framework is in place for its services.

So, instead of responding to external demands to measure the impact of their work, Crisis has developed its own internal drivers. Its board recognised that they themselves need to be able to understand how effectively the charity is delivering against its mission, in order to assess and set its strategic direction. They are aware that the context in which they work is constantly changing, and so any interventions which work well this year, may yet become obsolete quickly.

As a result Crisis has developed its own internal evaluation processes, which are linked to investment decisions in its strategic plan. Having a strong internal evaluation process is crucial for being able to assess the more, and less, effective activities and to focus more effort on what works. One result of this focus on mission and effectiveness has been that the charity is freed up to collaborate to achieve its objectives. "No matter how ambitious our strategy is, we cannot end homelessness on our own. So we want to embed in the system the interventions that really work". Jon Sparkes told me.

The charity is sharing policy and campaign work with smaller regional charities and is keen to develop a kind of sectoral knowledge exchange. They have also been instrumental in bringing homelessness charities together to campaign, for instance successfully lobbying with one voice on commitments for the 2019 general election. Because Crisis is assessing success against its mission more broadly, this opens up opportunities to re-invent itself and its response, enabling it to be entrepreneurial in the adoption of the best possible models to support people experiencing homelessness.

(Sparkes, 2020)

When I have asked job applicants why they are keen to work in a charity a fairly predictable majority will mention something about wanting to 'make a difference'. It is sometimes assumed that working for an organisation that has a charitable mission, and not profit, at its core, will directly result in a positive difference in society. But the reality is much more complex than that. Some have even suggested that this assumption can be damaging in itself: if we assume that any charity with a commendable mission is automatically having a good impact then we fail to challenge charities to do a better job of supporting their cause. We risk building in a sense of complacency in charities. It isn't enough for charities to exist for the right reasons, as sector commentator Sonia Sodha puts it "The social sector's mission should not mean that we take its effectiveness for granted" (Sodha 2016).

The Covid-19 support from the UK government was a salutary reminder that not everyone assumes that charities are doing a good job. In the immediate crisis of Covid-19, charities sought urgent help from the UK government. Despite warm words, this additional funding support for charities was agreed to only grudgingly, and when the government did agree to emergency funding it attempted to ringfence any cash to be used only on the most "essential" causes (HM Treasury 2020). This triggered a wave of indignation from charities not considered essential. As Andrew Purkis points out, many other services provided by charities such as smoking cessation support, community transport (ensuring vulnerable people are able to make hospital appointments) and respite work for carers for example, all sound like services that are essential, rather than simply 'nice to have' (Purkis 2020).

Charities clearly need to do more to demonstrate the positive difference they make, but the sheer range of charities and their very varied reasons for existing mean that they end up taking widely differing approaches. This is compounded by the different ways in which impact measurement is understood. Whereas it is mostly understood in the charity sector to be a necessary evil, a function of accountability to funders, in fact impact measurement is a vital tool for charities' own learning, as Crisis has shown.

Set Up To Fail?

Although all charities have a stated public benefit, the outline of what they hope to achieve is communicated in their mission statement. The crafting of mission statements is the focus of much attention and energy in the charity sector, all charities are expected to have one and they are intended to inspire funders, volunteers and staff. Primarily they are a clear way of collectively agreeing and then articulating what the charity stands for, so that all stakeholders can feel enthusiastic about supporting it. In their mission statement, charities will articulate their focus on improving lives within the existing context ('relief' charities) and/ or on solving problems ('prevention').

These public statements which a charity makes about its ultimate aims will often be extremely ambitious. For example, Barnardo's states:

> Our vision is to realise Thomas Barnardo's dream of a world where no child is turned away from the help they need.
>
> *(Barnardo's 2020)*

This boldness is engaging and inspiring for volunteers and donors, but it also presents a risk. It prompts us to ask the question: has the charity succeeded? If so, why does it continue to exist? And if not, then is it not effective? These questions are more pertinent the older the charity. One could ask after all, if Barnardo's has already had 175 years to end neglect and abuse of children and it still hasn't succeeded, is it time to call it a day? Similarly, is it reasonable to ask whether, as

Crisis has been running its services since the 1960s, and over the last decade street homelessness has significantly increased, then has the charity failed?

Of course, charities are relatively small players in a complex system. The resource that they can devote to solving these major social issues is tiny compared with the activities of the state and the private sector, and the financial scale at which charities operate is not commensurate with the scale of their stated ambitions (Gugelev and Stern 2015). But if charities are not achieving their missions in total then how do we know they are making a positive difference at all? This requires some evaluation of the alternative and understanding the counter-factual: what might the world have been like had Crisis or Barnardo's not run their services? This evaluation is something that the charity sector struggles with, as MacAskill sets out (MacAskill 2015: 70). Over the years a whole world of measurement has grown up to attempt to bridge this gap and provide some meaningful evaluation for charities, funders and donors.

How to Measure 'Good'?

Measuring how well charities perform against their missions is a complex undertaking. Businesses have a neat shorthand way of demonstrating effectiveness through cash. Money can immediately highlight profitable activities, expose loss-making initiatives, and help with planning resourcing by calculating margins and return on investment. It is a consistent standard, allowing comparison of companies across a range of different financial measures. Companies use this to evaluate the performance of individual aspects of their companies, including internal departments (using internal transfer values), and even the performance of individual members of staff (through sales figures, for example).

This just doesn't work in the charity sector. Charities do think in cash terms of course – the attention of CEOs and boards is usually, anxiously, fixed on cash flow and reserves – but cash does not tell even part of the story in a charity. It does not provide any measure of how well a charity is performing against its aims (its mission). A charity with a huge surplus can ring alarm bells in the non-profit sector, where in the private sector it would usually be a simple matter of celebration. Charities which make money are failing if they are not having a positive impact on their beneficiaries, and are seen as ineffective if they build up massive unspent reserves, rather than spending this on their cause. On the other hand, charities that lose money could still be running brilliant interventions that save lives.

Charities also lack the direct feedback loop which for-profit companies have through cash measures. A company quickly starts to lose money if its products are not good enough. For charities this is rarely the case because the person at the receiving end of a service or product is not the one paying for it – the donor or charitable foundation or commissioner is. But that third party (the donor or the funder) does not have any direct contact with the recipient, so the only way they get to know whether their money is being used effectively is through the charity.

The funder relies on reports supplied by the charity to understand the difference their investment is making. This has made the question of what these reports should be, and how effectively they measure the difference made, or impact, an increasingly hot topic in the sector. It does also mean that charities' primary motivation in adopting impact measurement tends to be to please a funder and to attract future funding, which in turn influences the nature of the measurement and reporting undertaken.

A vast amount has been written on the subject of impact measurement, so I don't intend to rehearse it all here. Historically the tendency has been for this reporting to simply offer proof that charities were delivering the activities they said they would, rather than evidence of these activities actually making a difference. So, for example, in my CEO roles I have been asked by funders to report back on the number of attendees at events, the number of service users on mailing lists (which was no indication they read anything we sent them, or indeed that the addresses on our system were up to date), and the number of enquires received by phone or email (a high number was assumed to be good, when in fact it could be a sign of confusing communications, which service users wanted to clarify). These numbers alone told funders nothing about the charity and its effectiveness, but they served to reassure busy grants officers that the charities were at least delivering some activities. The tendency remains for funders to fall back on something that is countable, but which may not be in any way meaningful, also known as 'vanity metrics'.

Impact Measurement

It is to combat these vanity metrics that charities and funders have, over recent years, explored new ways of measuring what they do in non-financial terms, through a huge array of different tools and techniques. Many charities have now articulated 'theories of change' which set out the ultimate impact the charity wants to make, the activities they undertake to achieve this and the milestones along the way. The model allows charities to track the intervention logic in their work, understanding how, or whether, the activities they deliver will have the outcomes they aim for and then how these outcomes will contribute to the change, the eventual impact, they want to see. The milestones set out in the theory of change are helpful points for measuring how the charity is progressing towards the impact it aims to achieve. Charities have also explored ways of linking a charity's value to monetised 'social returns on investment' (SROI) developed by economists and consultants to capture the long-term value of a charity's intervention.

As a result, there are now many different ways of capturing impact for charities, but no one single standard. This makes the measurement of impact a huge challenge for charities, especially smaller ones. Identifying meaningful milestones and then measuring progress can be difficult and expensive. Few people in small to mid-sized charities have the research skills or the time to set up robust impact measures and then to analyse the results (Ainsworth 2020). So this type of impact measurement can depend on paying for external consultants to support the charity, a costly process and one which a charity may not be able to sustain. In addition to being resource-intensive, the requirement to develop individual measurement also prevents charities from being benchmarked, so that they and their funders are able to assess their relative effectiveness.

Through my work at Heart of the City, I saw businesses grapple with similar issues. Increasingly investors are looking for companies to invest in that demonstrate a positive impact on society and the environment (termed ESG investing). This means they are seeking reliable measures of this impact in the business world. This isn't entirely new in the private sector, for more than ten years the corporate social responsibility (CSR) world has tried to find objective measures of the positive impact a company has, alongside its profit. This has resulted in some very detailed and extremely complex measures, such as the London Benchmarking Group, the Triple Bottom Line and the FTSE's Responsibility 100 Index. However, CSR work has historically been somewhat siloed in most companies. The development of ESG is a much more powerful driver of change in business, as it connects to the profit-making, investment-seeking core of the company. A lack of consistent measures has led individual investors to demand different sets of reports from companies, leading many to set up whole departments of specialists simply to deal with this as a 'compliance' issue.

Already accountancy firms and international investment groups have identified this lack of standardisation as a major weakness, which does not allow investors to make comparisons across sectors or companies, and there are urgent drivers for a single global standard measurement. It is likely the market will drive the development and adoption of a single standard very soon (Magor 2019). This measurement is complex and remains subjective, but it's been instructive to see the speed of progress on this in the private sector compared with the charity sector. Although charities started much earlier, the drivers for adoption and standardisation of measures have not been strong enough for this to be embedded in their work. As commentator David Ainsworth says, the "impact revolution has not fully taken hold. Many in the sector appear to view it with suspicion" (Ainsworth 2020). At this rate charities may find themselves in the peculiar position of the private sector reaching a set of value measures for non-profit-making activities before charities do. If they do so, this will be because private companies' drivers are stronger: for them, impact is much more closely linked to investment.

Funding Heroes to Rescue Victims

Where charities do measure their impact this tends to be driven by funder demands. Each funder will be asking the charity for different measures, based on their own objectives. Funders' reporting requirements will not (despite longstanding lobbying of the sector to be more standardised in their approach) be coordinated with other funders also trying to tackle the same issues. This can leave charities measuring and reporting on many different datasets and to a range of deadlines throughout the year. As a result it is not unusual to have to report results to different funders at several different points in the year. Numerous CEOs I spoke to were frustrated at the amount of administrative work this placed on their charity, which was disproportionate to the funding they received, and in particular was not reflected in the amount of funding received towards core costs (which pays for the resourcing necessary to set up data collection, to analyse and report results). Despite widespread recognition of this issue in the funding sector, progress on standardising reporting remains glacial. Some smaller and forward-thinking grant-makers, such as the corporate KPMG Foundation are taking a fresh approach – giving grantees the option of sharing with them existing measures being used for other grant-makers rather than gathering and reporting on new measures. Such a flexible approach sounds sensible but charities, loath to criticise or challenge their funder lifelines, lack the leverage to press funders to move faster on adopting a more consistent, standardised framework.

One CEO told me that family trusts and individual major donors were the most demanding but that her charity, like many, couldn't afford not to take grants because they were under pressure to diversify their funding (Interviewee T 2020). Even more worryingly, where funders do ask for burdensome reports, they still do not seem to be asking their grantees to measure meaningful data points with the aim of identifying and encouraging the most impactful projects. In fact the data that many funders collect too rarely seems to be used at all, beyond being stored as audit evidence of monies spent. One funder has courted controversy by speaking out against this culture in the grant-making sector. Mary Rose Gunn of The Fore told me that she felt charities, especially smaller to mid-sized charities, faced a completely disproportionate level of reporting requirements. Large funders could and should use data which was already available, such as annual reports, and that funders could use the same materials, rather than putting all the work on charities to produce multiple different sets of reports (Gunn 2020).

Peter Grant made a similar point to me, suggesting that funders and donors came in several different types and they should manage their demands for impact data accordingly, with some self-awareness. He described the 'Woodcutters' who want to see short term results; 'Artists' who don't worry about results, they just give; and 'Scientists' who want to see impact in the future. What was important about the categories was that the funder should be honest about what they are trying to achieve through their philanthropy:

> It is important to know which you are, really. Don't claim you are a scientist if you want to give out one-year grants! Don't make charities fill out impact reports if you're an artist.
>
> *(Grant 2020)*

Mary Rose Gunn also felt that often the relationship between funders and charities was unhelpfully transactional and wasn't focused on achieving long-term outcomes:

Many foundations are buying outcomes rather than investing in charities. This means charities turn themselves into organisations that sell outcomes/targets – skewed towards the issues that are in favour. They are forced to do this and are unable to invest in their own organisation or mission.

(Gunn 2020)

It is understandable that public funders may take a narrow view that they are required to 'buy' outputs alone (for example through commissioning a specific service provision). However, private funders have no such requirement and in both cases this narrowness of approach, failing to look to longer-term outcomes or to invest in the quality and development of the charity delivering these services, risks a drift into vanity metrics and, crucially, ineffective services. In her extensive interviews with people working in the sector, sector commentator Sonia Sodha heard similar views, with charity workers suggesting that funders aren't interested in people, just in projects:

It is unusual for funders to be interested in organisations, the people who work in the sector, and the knowledge that a particular project or activity may generate, after a grant comes to an end. Should they be?

(Sodha 2016)

Charities are incentivised to measure the impacts their funders seek, rather than those of their own mission. Caroline Fiennes of Giving Evidence explains that funders are drawn, unsurprisingly, to organisations that report success. This in turn incentivises charities to selectively publish their successes and not to publish any failures, it also encourages charities to overclaim their outcomes (Ainsworth 2020). Those I interviewed for this book expressed very similar concerns about the sorts of impact that funders wanted to see from charities. They spoke to me of an "old fashioned 'what's wrong?' approach" from many grant makers, a view articulated by CEO of Reach Volunteering, Janet Thorne:

Funders push us the wrong way by focusing on problem-solving. As a result, charities are incentivised to define their work in terms of a problem, and making those problems as large and simplistic as possible.

(Thorne 2020)

This encourages charities to cast their service users as victims and themselves as heroes. MP and former charity CEO Danny Kruger picked up on this in his report to the Prime Minister in 2020 (Kruger 2020: 16) and Sonia Sodha unearthed similar concerns: many sector workers felt uncomfortable that charities remained "too focused on needs and deficits, and not enough on empowering people to create positive change in their own lives". They were concerned that funding applications ask charities to evidence 'need' and fundraising campaigns play on images of need and vulnerability, and Sodha notes that "many charities are born out of the impulse to rescue people or fix an injustice" (Sodha 2016: 19).

Funders run the risk of investing in services that emphasise this sort of victimhood and paternalism. This can lead to the risk of charities having an unintentionally harmful effect on the people they are supposed to be supporting, by denuding them of a sense of agency over their own lives. As US academic Gregory Dees set out in his exploration of charity cultures, charity can be counterproductive, by robbing its beneficiaries of dignity and encouraging dependency (Dees 2012).

This is compounded by the timing of reporting on funding outcomes. Penny Wilson at Getting on Board recognised that an important issue with grant funding is that the projects funded 'need to work' and there is little opportunity to learn from failure and change tack partway through (Wilson 2020). Janet Thorne recounted the typical grant cycle:

> When charities apply for funding we have to show exactly how we will make a difference and to know in advance exactly what will happen. There is no option to change – we need to stick to the plan (even when it isn't working or the world has changed). Evaluation is when the project ends – when it's too late to change!
>
> *(Thorne 2020)*

This observation was echoed by Power to Change's Maitland Hudson, quoted in Civil Society News:

> If grant-makers were funding on the basis of reliable results, then you would expect to see cycles of funding that leave sufficient time to elapse for interventions to be established, data to be collected and analysed, and results published.
>
> *(Ainsworth 2020)*

However, she concludes "This isn't how funding operates".

This is a far cry from a robust process of evaluation, which should be designed in from the start of the charity's intervention and ideally also started at its outset. But, in my experience, the sort of summative, confirmatory evidence described by Janet Thorne is what is usually meant by a project evaluation. And what can we realistically expect, when charities do not secure additional funding, skills or assistance to carry this out? Thorne argues powerfully that this sort of culture pushes charities into a reductive mindset, which is a major curb on innovation:

> We should be iterating and evolving our core services, checking and improving them, taking a test and learn approach.
>
> *(Thorne 2020)*

But instead charities are stuck in a loop of "proving or certifying impact rather than informing improvements to practice" (Sodha 2016: 26).

Donor Demand For Impact

It is a truism in the charity sector that donors demand evidence of impact. In their research funded by the Charity Commission, Populus reported that individual donors were demanding evidence of impact, and the Commission drew the conclusion that providing this evidence would help restore trust in the sector. But I am not so sure. While members of the public might state this when asked, when it comes to giving there is little evidence that individual donor decisions, like major donor decisions, are based on objective weighing of data and effectiveness, and plenty of evidence that donors make emotional decisions (perhaps tacking on a little data to justify their gift) (Sanders and Tamma 2015).

The recent movement for effective altruism has made a compelling case for giving in an evidence-based way. It notes that much of charitable giving is based on an emotional response and points up the potential threats to charity effectiveness, which that causes. As William MacAskill sets out:

> We very often fail to think as carefully about helping others as we could, mistakenly believing that applying data and rationality to a charitable endeavour robs the act of virtue. And that means we pass up opportunities to make a tremendous difference.
> *(MacAskill 2015)*

For instance, donors are motivated to give to emergency appeals for emotional reasons and in direct proportion to the amount of media coverage a disaster secures, rather than in relation to the scales of its impact. This subjectivity is a point we have seen before, playing out in the types of causes donors choose to give to. Effective altruism makes a logical case for a much more objective approach to charitable donations, using data and evidence to identify the most damaging issues and the most effective mechanisms and vehicles for tackling those issues.

This emphasis on meaningful impact data is intended to result in donors pushing charities to do more and more meaningful impact measurement. However, as we have seen, this theory leaves out the reality of the psychology behind charitable giving and some of the very foundations on which charities are built. Whether we like it or not, emotion does have a role to play in the work of most charities and simply providing data and evidence of impact isn't automatically going to ensure that a charity secures high levels of donations.

So, neither grant funders nor individual donors are necessarily pushing charities to measure meaningful impact. However, there are plenty of reasons why good charities are, and should be, understanding the impact and effectiveness of their work. And they should be doing this primarily for their own ends, not for those of their funders.

Understanding Impact

I can see why many charity leaders, frustrated with reporting on meaningless proxies to funders, might wish they could ditch impact measurement and simply ask for a little more trust in the sector from grant makers. But charting and measuring impact are absolutely vital to charities' future, not simply in order to be accountable to funders but for their learning and development as organisations, as Crisis has shown. An understanding of, and commitment to, effectiveness should be an important spur to innovation, and it should provide the impetus to terminate ineffective interventions in favour of more effective ones. After all, how do charities know whether their work is making a difference, or whether in fact a different approach might be more affective, unless they are able to analyse impact evidence?

Even where charities have collected data in order to be accountable to their funders, they may not necessarily use this data for themselves. It is as if they are simply going through the motions for funders without getting to the heart of why they are collecting this data and understanding how it could help them (Sodha 2016). In addition, this data isn't widely shared. A charity CEO would find it difficult to find data to enable her to benchmark her charity's work and to uncover whether their particular youth mentoring service, for example, was achieving brilliant, average, or terrible results compared with other similar services. As David Ainsworth points out:

> The major problem is that evaluation and impact reports do not appear geared to presenting evidence which can be used to deliver better social outcomes in future.
>
> *(Ainsworth 2020)*

He refers to research by the London School of Economics' Julia Morley which looked into social impact reporting on 138 charity and social enterprise websites and found little evidence that this impact data was being used to deliver better results (cited in Ainsworth 2020). Very few charities make detailed information about the design and effectiveness of the interventions they deliver publicly available, making it difficult for anyone outside to understand whether these interventions are effective or not. The lack of comparable data across the sector means that we regularly miss the opportunity to improve services by comparing with others, and to weed out underperforming services.

The lack of robust, shared evaluations limits charities' opportunity to learn from others and to build on one another's successes. This process of continuous improvement does not take place in the charity sector because of the myriad different ways in which charities measure their services (even where they are seeking to achieve the same objectives) and because charities do not routinely share their data about what has worked and what has failed. It is also the case however that even where such information is available, it simply isn't in the culture of many charities to hunt it down, to digest and apply the learning they find.

A Learning Culture?

Although charting and understanding impact measurement can improve the effectiveness of charities, we should not underestimate the challenge for charities in embedding this in their work. As we have seen, funders' idiosyncratic reporting requirements can take charities' energy away from the task of collecting and analysing the data they need for their own learning. There is also the question of measurement skills and cost, as Caroline Fiennes points out, a proper measurement of impact is extremely complicated and expensive (Fiennes 2016). In addition, there is the question of culture: unfortunately this mindset of constant challenge and striving for improvement is not the natural mindset for many charities.

Kristina Glenn (former Cripplegate Foundation CEO) told me an anecdote that makes a similar point in a more flippant way: frustrated with colleagues in the charity sector routinely turning up 20 minutes or more late for meetings (a mysteriously widespread affliction in the charity sector) she decided to calculate the cost of the time of wasted by everyone else in the meeting waiting for them. Every member of staff's time is paid for by the charity they worked for and, as she well knows, salaries are most charities' highest cost. Reminding them that their time was valuable, and that it was time being paid for by their charity, she made the point that their time was a crucial resource; they should spend it wisely and they owed it to their beneficiaries to be on time (Glenn 2020).

Charities are not automatically incentivised to take seriously their responsibility to ensure they provide, not just *a* service or programme or project, but *the very best* intervention for the people they work with. This impetus to constantly improve is something that a well-functioning market can provide through competition and consumer demand in the private sector and, as we have seen, charities need to find their own equivalent of this.

When I spoke to charity leaders about their experience of reviewing the activities which their charity currently delivers against their charity's mission, most gave examples of recent strategic reviews or business-planning sessions. But digging deeper into these there was little appetite for the sort of searching review that deeply and regularly challenged the charity on what it was doing and why. Charity leaders may well be aware that their services could be better. They may have a nagging feeling that they are carrying old projects well past their sell-by date, but without either the push from funders, or the time (aka money) to review these and develop better projects they get stuck on this (not-so-)merry-go-round of funding/delivery/funding.

A slightly more tricky possible explanation for charity leaders not asking these searching questions is perhaps the fear of getting the 'wrong' answer. What if a genuine deep review of the charity's activities shows that it is not achieving its objectives? The psychological reasons behind a reluctance to ask this are obvious. By considering whether the charity might not actually be achieving its public benefit the charity's leader is looking into the abyss. Not only are they questioning the value of all they have invested in in terms of both effort, money and emotion, they are also considering the potentially huge question of re-imagining the charity, or even of whether the charity should continue to exist. At that point charity CEOs are imagining themselves and their staff team out of work, and trustees are contemplating something that feels like failure.

This brings us to consideration of the covert culture in charities. We know that unstated reasons may underlie the founding of charities, and that donors have unspoken reasons for giving to causes. These are emotional motivations and, whether we like it or not, emotion does have a large part to play in the formation and development of charities. Perhaps then, one reason that charity trustees and employees feel uninspired by measuring success is that they are emotionally attached to the work that the charity does and any challenge to that feels like a personal rejection.

After all, terminating longstanding services, which may be well loved by some trustees and service users (even if they are not effective or not helping the charity fulfil its mission) can feel traumatic. Writers talk about the process of axing beautiful, lyrical passages of prose which add absolutely nothing to character or plot as 'killing your babies'. Perhaps charities have something to learn from the difficult process of creative writing, where a critical review is painful, but it is essential to bringing a narrative to life. Similarly, ridding a charity of activities which do not contribute frees up times and resource to develop more effective new activities.

Asking Difficult Questions

A small number of charities have seriously challenged themselves about the difference they make, and questioned whether they are still needed in the current and future world. They have gone on to make a significant change to what they do. Understanding why they did this and how it helped them to achieve their charitable purpose could help us to understand the drivers that can push charities to plan for their future and the sort of context they need to be able to act on these.

CASE STUDY: SCOPE

Mark Atkinson's work at Scope is perhaps the best-known example of re-forming around mission in the charity sector. On taking over as CEO at Scope, Atkinson and the board of trustees undertook an unflinching review of what the charity did, evaluating the difference it made compared with its mission. What they discovered was a charity that had moved away from a clear focus on the difference it aimed to make, which had happened in a gradual evolving of the charity's work over many years.

Scope has its roots in campaigning families who fought in the 1950s for their children to get access to education and who set up their first schools for kids with disabilities, to prove that it could be done. In the years that followed the

---

charity grew up with those children: when they left the school Scope had set up there was no secondary school option available to them, so they set this up next. Later, on leaving school, there were no jobs and no supported housing suitable for the grown-up children and so the charity went on to provide a whole-life set of interventions, modelled on the needs of these children. These model services later led to the charity taking on and running services for local authorities and, by 2016, they were delivering multi-million pound contracts across the country.

The drivers for change in 2016 were both financial – as despite its major contracts the charity was struggling to cover its core costs – and also a lack of impact. Despite all its work the charity wasn't able to demonstrate that it was having a positive impact in line with its founding mission:

"We won't stop until we achieve a society where all disabled people enjoy equality and fairness".

When Atkinson and his board re-examined what they were delivering and compared this with their actual mission they felt that the activities that Scope was delivering were not helping to achieve this mission. Over time, the mission and the charity had moved apart. The quality of the services Scope delivered were fine, but were they really the kind of ground-breaking service the charity had originally been set up to pioneer? Were its services best-in-class and inspiring commissioners to run similar quality services elsewhere? In addition, the financial and resource-burden of delivering these low-cost services for commissioners was leaving the charity with little discretionary funding to use for new activities or non-statutory services.

With all this in mind Scope trustees took the decision that, where the present activities of the charity were not delivering the charity's strategy, they would be handed over to other providers to run. This is a decision that few other charities have made. This led Scope to a massive reduction of two-thirds of staff and 40% of turnover, as well as the transfer of its regulated services to a for-profit provider. It cleared out old services and freed up time and resource to be focused more closely on achieving the charity's mission. But it also attracted negative headlines from across the charity press.

(Atkinson 2019)

Breathless headlines about the reduction in Scope's turnover, and the fact that their contracted services were handed over to private sector companies continue to pop up (Kay 2020). Both areas of implied criticism give us some useful insights into why more charities do not undertake, and act on, reviews like this. These headlines completely miss the point about charities: the aim of charities is to fulfil their mission, not to continue legacy services at all costs, they are not there to prevent local authority services from being run by private contractors and charities should not aim simply to grow their turnover. It also points up the tension between a charity's responsibility to its employees which, contrary to popular feeling across the sector, does in fact come second to a charity's responsibility to its beneficiaries.

Having a large turnover does not make a charity more effective, this is simply an aspect of the work that is measurable and comparable and it does not reflect the success or otherwise of delivery against mission. Scope could have continued to run services at a break-even level and it would have remained busy, it would then have retained its higher level of turnover, but the trustees' evaluation of these services demonstrated that they were not helping the charity to fulfil its mission. In which case, continuing to devote its resources to these services would mean its trustees being negligent in their responsibilities, as they would not be using their resources in the best way to achieve their mission.

Atkinson is animated on the idolisation of growth in the charity sector. He strongly believes that charities need to 'subtract to multiply', that is they should first stop the activities which are not contributing to their mission, before they can really increase their impact. This is also a view articulated by Gugelev and Stern, practitioners in US non-profit incubators and foundations, who concluded that very few non-profits are able to achieve the scale commensurate with the size of the social challenges they seek to overcome (Gugelev and Stern 2015). Charities should be less concerned with growing turnover and absolutely obsessed with growing impact. For Scope, income growth was a red herring, impact was the real aim, and in order to achieve that impact the charity needed to dramatically change what it did. At Scope the drivers of change were a lack of impact and a lack of funding, creating a burning platform of sorts (Atkinson 2018).

Without a burning platform (i.e. a crisis) it may be difficult for charity leaders and trustees to contemplate a radical change. Yet, conversely, when there is a burning platform (e.g. drastic loss of funding) it is difficult for anyone, trustees or staff, to have the headspace and time to come up with a truly transformative plan. This seems to be a crucial factor in preventing innovation in the sector. Making use of data on charities' performance however has the potential to enable charities to create a longer-term, considered change and a gradual adaptation and improvement in services. It can help charities to understand how effectively they perform against the ambitious missions they set themselves; it could also enable them to collaborate with other charities. Meaningful evaluation data could help charities to compete more effectively by disrupting charities' assumptions about the effectiveness of their work; it could encourage charities to be more transparent about their learning, and it should, through all of this, lead to a better standard of services for the people and causes that charities are set up to support.

Competition

Competition is a dirty word in the charity sector. Charities don't like to admit that the services they provide are in any way similar to those of any other charity, and the public and funders seem to find the idea of competition between charities distasteful. However, the truth is that charities are fiercely competitive, they are pushed into constant competition with one another for scarce funding resources. Charities delivering similar services approach the same commissioners and the same charitable trusts. They also target the same demographic groups to woo individual donors.

Where competition is intense in the charity sector innovation can thrive. this can be seen in the creative and speedy ways in which fundraisers adapt their tools and techniques in response to new technology (e.g. crowd-funding or text giving) and new regulations (e.g. the Fundraising Regulator). But fundraising isn't where the innovation is needed. As Kurt Hoffman, former CEO of the Institute for Philanthropy, said:

> When the best and brightest working in the charity sector are spending so much time fundraising, this happens at the expense of devoting conscious effort to innovating and improving performance—which is by far the most important source of value creation in every other product sector in our economy.
>
> *(Hoffman 2013)*

The other common element of competition in the sector can drive a race to the bottom: Commissioners commonly award contracts in ways which prioritise price over quality, depressingly they frequently state a weighting of 80% on price and 20% on quality in tenders for adult social care contracts. As a result charities can find themselves in competition with one another and with the private sector to deliver the lowest unit cost on contracts. While price can drive some degree of innovation, in my experience running commissioned services allows very little, if any, space for developing excellence in services. Too many charities find themselves caught in the bind of servicing ever-more onerous contracts which draw them further away from the charitable work, and which offer little contribution to core costs in any case. This is an especially acute issue for smaller charities that lack the brand, experience and leverage to negotiate on pricing and standards (Lloyds Bank Foundation 2016). Too often we see charities forced to compete on prices for contracts that they just can't deliver. As a result they end up subsidising these contracts with their other funded income (NPC 2020:16).

Charities are competing, whether we like it or not. The problem is, they are competing on the wrong things. As Kurt Hoffman points out, charities would benefit from expending more of their attention and innovation on developing the best services rather than the best fundraising methods. Competing on impact would enable them to do this. By undertaking higher quality evaluations, and by using and sharing this data to learn, more and less effective charities would be visible not just to funders, but also to trustees. Benchmarking would help to ensure that investment tipped towards the better interventions, but more than this being just a question of funding, this would help teams internally to improve services, and to focus resources on where they are most effective.

Paradoxically, competing on effectiveness could also help charities to collaborate with others. Although the sector talks up collaboration and funders have tried to push charities to collaborate more, for years this hasn't resulted in major breakthroughs. This is because charities' drivers all point in the other direction. As Kania and Kramer set out, this failure to collaborate is wasteful:

> nearly 1.4 million [US] nonprofits try to invent independent solutions to major social problems, often working at odds with each other and exponentially increasing the perceived resources required to make meaningful progress.
>
> *(Kania and Kramer 2011: 38)*

However, they go on to identify the barriers that charities face in collaboration, which range from managerial skills to the lack of shared impact measurement tools, to funding for backbone support organisations and, crucially, the long-term and patient support of funders (Kania and Kramer 2011). As a result charities tend to slide into what they term 'individual impact' as opposed to the 'collective impact' that they see as crucial to tackling complex and interrelated social issues which require multiple stakeholders' involvement to tackle.

Carolyn Housman, CEO of Children and Families Across Borders, articulated the challenge that many charities experience around collaboration:

> Charities have their own missions, their reasons for existence, and believe in this mission over and above that of another charity. As a result, they often will need too much of the limelight for themselves, in order to raise awareness for their own cause. There is an uncomfortable balance to be struck between pushing forward your own charity's mission, as this is the job you are hired to do, and collaborating with others, as we often believe this is one of the features that distinguishes us from the private sector. Then there is the complicating factor that funding is dependent on showing attribution: we need to prove that we, our charity, alone made the difference. Trustees have hired me, as CEO, to innovate and grow the charity in order to meet our charitable objectives – and they want to see this reflected in quarterly Board reports. Furthering the aims of another charity alone just wouldn't cut it.
>
> *(Housman 2020)*

As the Crisis example shows, a more objective focus on what is best for the charity's cause, a sense of an 'endgame' (Gugelev and Stern 2015) or focus on collective action (Kania and Kramer 2011), rather than on preserving its current activities and income at all costs, has the potential to free up charities to explore different methods of achieving our mission. Collaboration has huge potential to enable charities to make a far greater difference.

Making a Difference in the 2020s and Beyond

The demands placed on charities to show that they are making a positive difference will only increase. With businesses increasingly able to quantify and compare their non-cash performance, charities will have to adapt or dwindle. Funders will ask for more transparency over what they get for their money and individual donors will expect this too in shift towards 'radical transparency' (Cordery, Smith and Berger 2017). Charities that cannot or will not provide this, or those that try to hide their true costs, will be exposed. Those charities which step forward and clearly set out their real costs and the real benefits will be the winners.

There are reasons for optimism in this. The world does still look to non-profits for answers and I was struck by Banergee and Duflo's *Good Economics for Hard Times*, where the economists cited non-profit projects as the most effective responses to some of the social challenges they identify. And how did they know with confidence that the charity projects were effective? Because the projects assessed their impact using evidence based as closely as possible on randomised controlled trials (RCTs), the gold standard for scientific research (Banergee and Duflo 2019). The impact of the projects Banerjee and Duflo examine was measured as objectively as possible in a standardised test that is universally recognised as robust.

Of course, RCT-level evaluations aren't practical for many non-profit interventions and we should not expect charities to adopt disproportionately complex methods of measurement. But we should also recognise that using impact testing of high quality like this opens the door to a whole new world of standardised review, project sharing and collaborative work. Similarly, high quality theory-based approaches can provide strong evidence of impact and aid learning in areas where context is crucial and where more nuanced outcomes are sought. All of these approaches however do need to be resourced, and it is essential that funders who genuinely aim to have impact do cover the full cost of charities' work to understand the effectiveness of their interventions.

Data shared on non-profit interventions holds out the tantalising prospect of pilot projects being shared and emulated and applied in similar environments in very different countries and cultures. This replication could enable non-profits with effective interventions to see these applied on a scale that any individual charity would struggle to achieve. In the world of social science, peer-reviewed journals provide a helpful way of both badging the quality of research and of sharing research findings. At present any such research into the outcomes of charity interventions is rare and, where it does exist, it would be published in subscription journals, which are not regularly accessed by those in operational roles in the charity sector.

Stronger impact measurement, which focuses on the charity's mission itself rather than diluting its work across reporting different measures to multiple different funders, may better enable charities to attract investment from new sources, with investors prizing impact over profit. It may even open up the possibility of peer-reviewed journals sharing and assessing the effectiveness of differing interventions, helping to shine a light on ground-breaking practice and encourage excellence as well as dissemination. The prize then is great. By looking to the future charities have an opportunity now to use impact to develop the projects that will really help them to achieve their ambitious missions and underline their relevance in the coming decades.

4

HOW SHOULD CHARITIES BE FUNDED?

CASE STUDY: CHILDREN AND FAMILIES WITHOUT BORDERS

Children and Families Without Borders (CFAB) is a small charity with a big reach. From its office in central London the international charity supports children being reunited with their families and has helped tens of thousands of families in 120 countries since it was founded. To fund its work CFAB secures funding from nearly 100 local government departments, several central UK government departments, charitable funders and individual donors.

CFAB has an annual turnover of only £760,000 (2019) but, like many charities its size, its finances are surprisingly complex. In 2019 12 of the charity's funders placed restrictions on how the charity could spend their grant. This meant the charity had to know in advance how it would need to spend the money, so the funding could not necessarily be used as it was needed as circumstances changed. Also, importantly, the mere management of all these funding streams created a significant, additional administrative burden as each grant has to be managed carefully through the charity's accounts. Each bundle of funding, some as little as £2,000, must be disaggregated again at the end of any reporting period to show that CFAB has spent each budget as their funders required. This means an accountant having to run period-end reports separately to the charity's main accounts, in addition to helping check the spend down of the budget in the year. Each year is a complex balancing act to ensure that the charity secures enough from each project to cover the charity's core costs which keep it functioning, including paying for the accountant (Housman 2020).

DOI: 10.4324/9781003139089-4

The complexity of CFAB's funding is far from unusual in the charity sector. One of the fundamental challenges faced by charities is the nature of their funding. Because charities' activities are not paid for by the people who use them, each charity instead has to raise the money they think they need to run a service from other sources. The sources will vary, from individual donors to charitable trusts, wealthy philanthropists, local authorities or other statutory services, but the funder will be the one to decide whether this particular service run by this charity is what is needed for the beneficiary. Not the beneficiary herself.

This is the challenge at the root of charity funding. It creates an imperfect market where funding fails to flow naturally to the causes, the geographical areas and the organisations that are most needed by any objective assessment of the facts. Instead the amount and nature of funding secured relies on the funding strategy of the charity and its ability to persuade funders to choose it, to believe in it, to trust it to deliver.

As we'll see, different funders want to see different things from the charities they fund, and so charities can find themselves dancing around in a frenzy of reporting requirements, balancing of short-term funding and self-promotion in a bid to meet the conflicting expectations of their various tune-callers. Funders' requirements also tend to focus on the needs of beneficiaries, which in turn pushes charities to portray, and also to perceive, their beneficiaries in a certain way: as victims, as passive recipients of a service. This has profound implications on the power relationships between funders and charities and the people and causes they are supposed to be there to support.

'Assets, Assets Everywhere and We Can't Make Payroll This Week'

The traditional view of charities sees organisations funded simply by individual donors and, perhaps, charitable foundations. The reality for charities today is very different. Charities are funded from multiple sources, which can fluctuate enormously and which come with a number of different strings attached. Balancing these streams of income to secure the amount of funding required is challenging because of the problem of super-illiquidity that afflicts charities. Clara Miller describes this illiquidity taking Coleridge's Rime of the Ancient Mariner as her inspiration:

> "Assets, assets everywhere, and we can't make our payroll this week." Donor restrictions on either assets or income, coupled with the nature of the asset, create risk and expense because they are more likely to create demands on capacity and program beyond what the donor originally envisioned and what may have been planned for by the nonprofit.
>
> *(Miller 2003: 5)*

This problem of illiquid, restricted funding is ubiquitous in the charity sector. This is where funders, and often individual (major) donors, place additional restrictions on how the charity can spend the money they give. This is what leads to the situation at CFAB as in almost all charities, where the streams of charitable funding can only be spent on certain items and within certain time periods. Every penny of that restricted income has to be accounted for separately, which means charities keeping and logging different budgets to ensure that they spend down the restricted funding to the correct timescales. If they do not do this there is a risk the funder could ask for their unspent money back (although in my experience it is rare for funders to do this, except in cases of fraud, which begs the question whether this is in fact a meaningful and proportionate control for funding spend).

This restricted funding does not, on the face of it, sound very attractive from a charity point of view. Individually, these pots of restricted funding can be very small and each requires resource to manage, but most charities feel that they have no choice but to accept this. However, despite the fact that restricted funding often only allows a charity to charge a small amount towards the core costs of the organisation, these small contributions are often vital to funding the elements that keep the charity going: an accountant, an IT system, phone lines, office rental and receptionist, as well as for management roles. As one charity CEO told me:

> We don't have much choice about who take money from. We can't afford to just choose trusts that give core funding or support investment in staff and infrastructure as it's essential to diversify funding.
>
> *(Interviewee T)*

Diversify or Die

The Carers Network is a charity that started as an informal support group for local unpaid carers in the 1990s set up by the carers themselves. It started to receive local authority grant funding and set itself up as a registered charity. As funding arrangements changed after 2010, local grants were gradually phased out and the local council, like many across England, instead invited the charity to apply for a contract to deliver a service, which the council itself specified. The charity duly did this but the trustees were rightly mindful of a concentration of funding from the state, which was also reducing its available funding to focus on essential services. It was in a bid to diversify its funding that the charity sought new sources of income to reduce this dependence and to support a wider range of services to meet the needs of informal carers. By 2017 (when I worked there) the charity had evolved to be funded by a mix of public contracts, charitable grants, merger income, corporate donations and a small block of individual donations.

This evolution of funding to a blended model is a journey that many charities have taken over the last 10 to 15 years. Many charities continue to diversify funding so they are not dependent on one single funder. This means they are able to survive if one funder withdraws money, or if that funder's requirements are no longer compatible with the charity's mission.

CASE STUDY: MAKING THE LEAP

Tunde Banjoko, CEO of Making the Leap, experienced first-hand the risk of over-concentrated funding when 70% of his funding disappeared overnight. Making the Leap had been 100% public sector funded, but when the London Development Agency was dissolved the charity was left with just 30% of their usual funding. After years of having positive and supportive relationships with their public sector funders the charity had not needed to find alternative or complementary funding. The loss of funding forced them into a speedy pivot in which they reinvented the charity, bringing trading income into the mix for the first time through a national awards scheme. Seven years on, the small charity has a large profile and stable, diverse funding in place thanks to significant commitment from staff and some very creative thinking

(Banjoko 2020).

Since 2010 the charity sector has seen dramatic changes in the types of funding available to it. The squeeze on government grants in particular has pushed charities to diversify their funding sources and funders have placed a huge emphasis on developing new areas of income generation such as contract income and trading income. However, as they developed new sources of income charities haven't brought public expectations with them. The public still tends to think of charities as being funded by donations, it seems that they do not expect charities to be trading or delivering public contracts and, when they see charities displaying some of the characteristics required of them for these more commercial type of operations (such as funding infrastructure support, compliance and specialist staff) they feel less trusting of charities and what they do (Populus and Charity Commission 2018). This funding mix, whilst necessary to charities' survival, may contribute to undermining the public's trust in the charity sector.

Individual Donors

Individual donors remain the single largest source of funding for charities in England and Wales (NCVO 2020), and this is also the type of funding with which the general public is most familiar and is most comfortable. However, these donations are not spread evenly. Donations are based on the personal preference of donors, as we have seen ('cats and cancer'), rather than on data about the causes and geographical areas where there is the greatest need. But in addition to individual donor preference there is another important factor at play here. That's investment in fundraising, because donors do not decide to make donations in a vacuum.

While other areas of charity development have struggled to innovate, fundraising continues to develop new channels to reach individual donors. There are many familiar methods of securing donations, from sponsored races to direct mail-shots to fundraising events and securing bequests in wills. In recent years, larger charities developed their email marketing and text donations, while even smaller charities dabbled in crowdfunding. Charity fundraisers routinely use digital marketing and advertising where charities' operational teams have been slower to adopt digital methods for service-delivery. That is largely because of the returns: good fundraisers are aware of the ratios behind their fundraising investments and they are also aware that some of their older, reliable sources of fundraising are less and less effective, as returns on investment are expected to reduce further (Institute of Fundraising 2019b: 29). Chugging (street marketing of charity direct debits) and direct marketing continue, but are more heavily regulated, and returns on investment (ROIs) for direct marketing appeals have reduced, as data protection rules limit contact lists and compliance with regulation adds operational cost.

All of these fundraising methods cost money. Even crowdfunding requires significant communications support to drum up interest from donors, to analyse and target networks, to craft an inviting project for investment, and pay for hosting. Direct marketing campaigns are hugely expensive and legacy fundraising campaigns take a significant upfront investment for a very long-term pay-off. So, individual donor fundraising significantly favours the charities with cash to invest, and it is no surprise then that the largest charities with the most money also invest an enormous amount in fundraising. The likes of Cancer Research UK and Battersea Dogs and Cats Home invest heavily in adverts, direct marketing, chugging, fundraising events and highly lucrative will-writing services. Cancer Research spent more than £100m on raising funds in 2019 alone and this pays off: it has built, and it maintains, a household-name status (Cancer Research UK 2019). Super-major charities like this have recognisable brands, which means that they are front-of-mind when you and I think about which charity to nominate for sponsorship in an event, or which charity to give to at Christmas. In turn this helps donors feel comfortable with giving to large charities whose brand they recognise, thinking of them as a known quantity.

Legacy fundraising is a clear example of this. Large charities recognised the potential for bequests for fundraising and developed free charity will-writing services to encourage people to include a bequest to their charity when writing their will (Sproson 2020). For those charities which could afford to offer this, the investment has paid off: over the five years to 2019 legacy income was the highest growing area for charity income, seeing a 50% increase, but that additional income went almost exclusively to the largest UK charities (those with more than £10m in annual income) (Institute of Fundraising 2019b: 25).

While these lucrative fundraising ROIs have worked for the largest charities, they present a barrier to entry for less wealthy charities. With the same charities always able to out-spend their poorer peers, the same charities continue to occupy the top ranks for income: the more money they manage to fundraise the more they can invest in raising more money, which can be ploughed back into fundraising, and so on. For the vast majority of charities these sorts of investments are completely unrealistic. Without a recognisable brand, smaller charities rely on word-of-mouth marketing and crowdfunding and raise relatively small sums from individual donors.

This stasis is significant because it prevents disruption amongst the major charities. Of all the 32 charities with an income of over £100m in 2018 none was formed after the 1980s (those later additions are simply mergers of longstanding charities such as Age UK – formerly Age Concern and Help the Aged) (NCVO 2018). This means that the charities with the highest levels of income were set up to tackle, at their most recent, the causes that mattered 30 years ago. Whilst those causes do still exist (cancer, or an ageing population for instance) it is significant that not one single new charity, set up to tackle emerging issues since the 1980s, has managed to break into this list of the so-called 'super-majors'. Fundraising costs and the related need to build brand recognition are major reasons why this oligopoly of top charities endures.

Besides the costs of generating individual donations, there are new challenges ahead for all charities wishing to develop this line of income in the future. Even before the Covid-19 crisis decimated major areas of giving such as events and sponsorship, charitable fundraisers were already warning of a stagnation or a contraction in fundraising even amongst the largest charities (Institute of Fundraising 2019a: 11). Interestingly, the Institute of Fundraising (IoF) identifies organisational inertia and lack of innovation and future-proofing throughout the sector as being at the heart of fundraisers' concerns. Despite the higher level of innovation in fundraising compared with other aspects of charity work, the IoF's interviewees sounded alarm bells about a diminution of investment in the broader strategic development in charities (Institute of Fundraising 2019a: 18).

If strategic development stagnates in a charity overall, the ability of fundraisers to upgrade income generation is limited. Digital engagement has been exposed as being one major area where charities have fallen behind not just businesses but also social enterprises. Report after report has bemoaned charities' slow adoption of digital strategy. Digital channels and software are used by charities where these provide a cheaper alternative to existing options, and certainly the shift to remote working through Covid-19 has accelerated this change. However, crucially, charities have not as a rule critically reviewed what they do and how they do it through the lens of digital capability.

Fundraisers have innovated as far as they can, but the IoF report states that they need to see a broader shift in organisational culture towards digital in order to take fundraising to the next level. This is because of a change in donor expectations: donors increasingly want to be involved in a conversation with the charities they support, and simply asking them for money will not be enough any longer. The IoF interviewees point out that charities need to reinvent themselves as modern, responsive organisations which engage with their donors and their beneficiaries, and digital engagement is essential to achieving this (Institute of Fundraising 2019a: 24).

This issue of responsiveness to donors raises an important point about the structural challenge that charities face in innovation, which is not limited to fundraising:

contemporary audiences have expectations shaped by the digital world around them. They increasingly expect organisations to be responsive to them, to engage with them on their own terms and to provide a personalised experience. Few charities have managed to adapt to this so far. In a survey of charities for The Future Charity report 62% reported that their organisation struggled to meet supporter expectations by delivering an effective digital experience and, among those respondents, 53% blamed poor organisational culture, and 47% an inability to recruit requisite skills (Massive, Kivo and Manifesto, 2019: 18). Businesses have had to develop this capability in order to connect with their customers, but charities, because of their peculiar and indirect funding structure (where the donor/funder pays for the service, not the recipient) have not had the impetus to adapt and develop the responsive and personalised services that will appeal to both the beneficiaries and the individual donors of the present and future. Moreover, the constraints on their ability to invest in the appropriate skills means that charities may also struggle to buy in the digital analytics expertise they need to develop these services.

Public Funding

For many charities operating in the areas of greatest need, public sector funding is the only option, as the necessary donors and charitable trusts may not exist in some of the most disadvantaged areas of the country. Analysis carried out before the 2008 financial crisis and mapping the subsequent public spending cuts showed that the charities in areas with the highest levels of deprivation in England and Wales had the highest level of public sector funding (Clifford 2017). Across the charity sector as a whole, public funding (from the health service, central and local government and other statutory agencies) has always been a component of charities' income, in contrast to the public's understanding of charity funding. However, since 2003/4 the nature of this funding has shifted from grant funding to contracts.

Whereas in 2003/4 the level of contract and grant income from central and local government was fairly equal (£5.8bn in contract funding, £6.1bn in grants), from that point onwards the type of funding began to diverge rapidly. Ten years later grants made up just £2.5bn in funding and a huge £12.5bn was administered through contracts (House of Lords 2017: 41). Many local authorities ran grant programmes for charities up until 2010. Since then, the pressure to deliver only what they are statutorily required to has driven many local authorities to offer contracts to charities instead. They are contracting out those services that they are legally required to deliver (for example in social care) and local charities may apply to run these, alongside private sector competitors and national charities.

Bidding to deliver a contract is a very different consideration for a charity from applying for grant income and it presents many significant barriers to smaller charities (Lloyds Bank Foundation 2016). It is hardly surprising then, that since 2000 the share of the sector's income enjoyed by small to mid-sized charities has dramatically decreased, with increased contract funding being secured by large, and particularly the very large, charities (NCVO 2020). Smaller charities (with an income of less than £500,000) suffered most through the shift to a model of commissioning, as Lloyds Bank Foundation has shown. These charities overall saw a 20% reduction in their income levels and a significant shift away from government funding to individual donations (Lloyds Bank Foundation and NCVO 2013: 3).

There are several reasons for this. Contracts tend to be on a much larger scale and often they are only open to organisations with a turnover above a certain size. The complexity of overseeing contracts demands that an organisation has a certain level of infrastructure and skills. For instance, the charity will need to ensure that it manages the complex rules around data protection where case notes are shared between contractors, and it needs to be experienced enough to tackle common challenges from commissioners around funding restrictions and surpluses. The charity needs to be able to handle detailed and frequent financial and operational reporting and may also need to handle VAT chargeability correctly. For charities with a part-time accountant, no HR function or data protection expertise these all present major challenges.

As Lloyds Bank Foundation has shown in its sobering 2016 report *Commissioning in Crisis*, smaller charities can lack both the knowledge and the leverage to fight back when commissioners place additional requirements onto their contracts (Lloyds Bank Foundation 2016). The management of contracts can also add a huge amount of work to smaller charities. Moreover, moving to delivering contracts can also prompt a significant change in the culture of a charity. As Noel Hyndman puts it:

> Charities rely heavily on trust relationships and communal accountability, rather than market relationships and contractual accountability … a contract funding regime (as opposed to grants being made to support activity) may influence the culture and actions of those within a charity … [and] undermine a broader and more reflective … view of performance.
>
> *(Hyndman 2017)*

So, as charities start to deliver public services, meet unit costs and sometimes get paid through a payment-by-results model, they risk undermining the very culture that gives them value in the eyes of their stakeholders. They may become more focused on reaching funding targets than providing a quality support to their beneficiaries. They may also find themselves delivering services that they don't feel are in line with their mission.

CASE STUDY: WESTMINSTER CARERS

One unusual example of a charity which decided to wind down its service rather than continue to deliver a cut-cost version of its work was the former charity Westminster Carers. The charity was well-regarded across Westminster for providing respite care to unpaid carers. It prided itself on retaining its staff and providing a personalised service to households in some of the most disadvantaged and diverse wards in the capital. The same carers visited each household regularly and their pay was above the minimum wage. This enabled the charity to retain staff long term, so the carers built up strong relationships with the families they supported. However, when commissioners re-contracted the care service its value was reduced by 25% and it would require clients to move to a direct payments model. On weighing up the risks the trustees judged that it would have been impossible for them to provide a safe, high quality service with the funds available and that the business model was unsustainable. Reluctantly they decided to wind down the carers' service in 2014 and to transfer their remaining assets to another charity in 2016.

(Lien, Katerji and Griffiths 2020)

This financial pressure to reduce the cost (and therefore the quality) of services is far from an isolated example. Of charities surveyed by NPC for their 2020 *State of the Sector* report, 22% said that they delivered contracts that were outside their mission. Of small charities surveyed, 61% reported that they were cross-subsidising public sector contracts with their (precious) unrestricted funding, because the contracts did not pay enough to be viable when delivered at the standard required for the charity's mission (NPC 2020b: 14–16).

Sometimes charities have little choice but to continue with delivering contracts if they want to survive in any form. They may have no other funding options available and lack the power in their relationship with a large public sector funder to persuade them to change their services to be more in line with beneficiary needs. As NCVO explains:

organisations are 'mission-led' and for many, the option of 'walking away' from a contract is problematic, particularly if the contract is the only way of continuing to work with their beneficiaries.

(NCVO 2014b: 8)

Many charities continue with statutory services as a way of funding their core infrastructure. They may hope that the contracts do not take up all their team's energy, so they will be able to secure other complementary sources of funding to deliver the projects which they and their beneficiaries want and need. However, with powerful funders and demanding contracts to be delivered, there is a risk that the contracts absorb all the energy and attention of the charity and result in a drift away from its original mission. When a member of the public encounters a charity running poor and underfunded public services like this it can shape their view, not just of that charity but perhaps also of all charities – *why are they delivering such poor services? Why are we paying taxes to go to charities to run this? If they have council money then they don't need my donation…*

Not-So-Charitable Trust Funding

For charities unwilling to rely on public sector contracts and/or unable to attract individual donors, the option of funding from grant-making trusts remains. There are hundreds of grant-making foundations across England and Wales giving around £6.5bn per year (ACF 2019: 4), alongside many hundreds of other charitable trusts. Some are enormous and open, with grant application processes and criteria that anyone can see and consider applying for. Many more are shrouded in mystery: family funds which make grants by invitation only; wealthy liveries and guilds where criteria and application processes are opaque, and unstaffed trusts where a charity has to apply by letter to a solicitor in order to find out about the application process.

All trusts and foundations have their own distinct application processes and, for successful grantees, their own reporting and monitoring requirements. They each have their own set of causes to support, many of which are set out in the organisation's founding documents, but are sometimes re-purposed for contemporary relevance. For example, the John Ellerman Foundation's principle benefactor had a strong interest in maritime issues which today's board has re-interpreted with contemporary relevance, by funding activities to reduce environmental damage to marine habitats.

Unsurprisingly, charitable foundations report anecdotally that the demand for grants has shot up in recent years, further increasing competition amongst charities for precious funding. Even where charities are successful in securing grants however, the way in which these grants are traditionally constructed is causing increasing disquiet in the sector. Most trusts and foundations offer restricted funding. The idea behind restricted funding is very attractive to the funder because it gives the illusion of control. Let's say you want to support a national charity to deliver its excellent advice service in a town where you live, you could stipulate that your donation goes only to that service and not to the charity's campaigning work, nor to its policy work, nor to its fundraising costs, nor to its IT systems, marketing or any other area of its business.

But this restriction means that the charity is forced to segregate your funding from other funding. If it had a huge influx of funding for your local project, more than it needed, it would not be able to use that money for any other projects, but would have to keep carrying it forward in its accounts (or pay it back to you), even when it had other similar projects desperately in need of cash. It would not be able to spend any of that money on core infrastructure even if, say, it couldn't afford to maintain its IT system, which then meant that your local project suffered regular connection problems. It would not be able to use your donation to upgrade its website so that other people could find out about the project that you love locally. It also would not be able to spend your surplus money on developing the next generation of great projects to support people in need. Because it could only spend your money on that one, small, local project.

As Clara Miller explains, restricted funding is a fallacy and can even end up costing charities more money to deliver because:

> the manager needs to raise money to pay for costs the other funds don't cover in order to be able to fulfil the contract or grant terms. … ironically, many non-profit agencies can't afford to take the money, given the restrictions and the lack of funds to pay for all the necessities those restrictions rule out.
>
> *(Miller 2005)*

Such restrictions also rather miss the point of charities, failing to notice that charities are *already* restricted in their purpose. Every single registered charity has its mission locked into its work through its registered charity status, so any further restriction to a specific project is just tying the charity's hands. It indicates a lack of trust and a lack of understanding of how charities work in practice. Unfortunately for charities though, restricted funding remains a mainstay of grant funding. It has taken the Covid-19 crisis to finally shift many funders into offering unrestricted funding, we can only hope that once the immediate crisis recedes funders recognise that charities are able to deliver as well, or even better, by being trusted to spend grants as they see fit (Wilkins 2020).

The Burden of Overheads

Most restricted grants do allow for a limited amount of 'overheads' or 'admin' spend, but there is an expectation that this will be capped. Some charities themselves fetishise this low overheads figure. Comic Relief is a particularly prominent and unhelpful offender. Every year I wince when I see its headline claim that "100% of your donation goes towards helping those in need" because it further embeds this expectation in donors' minds. In fact, when you read the explanatory paragraph on its website, Comic Relief goes on to say that it does spend some of each donation on overheads because it "includes the cost of making sure that your donation is allocated to good projects and properly monitored and evaluated" (Comic Relief 2020). Of course it does.

This sort of sophistry only perpetuates the fiction that charities can survive and be effective with minimal overheads, and it further encourages donors to look to this as an indication of quality in a charity to give to. This is exactly the sort of thinking that the Charity Defense Council in the US has tackled head-on through their powerful billboard and education campaigns that challenge the assumption that overheads are detrimental to a charity's performance.

The amount which UK charities can claim from a restricted grant towards their core costs tends to be capped at around 10%. This is despite research showing that, in order to recoup the full costs of delivering their work, charities would need on average to charge for core costs at 15–20% of any restricted grant (comparing favourably with banks incidentally, which average a *c.*25–30% core cost requirement) (Cass Business

School undated.b). What is more, this 'overhead' cost actually correlates with greater effectiveness in charities: as Caroline Fiennes points out 'high-performing charities spend more on administration costs than weaker ones do' (Fiennes 2013).

The result of this restricted funding and aversion to paying for 'overhead' is the ongoing and significant underfunding of the core functions of a charity. That is why charity websites are likely to be irritatingly clunky and out of date; it is why charities may be so slow to respond to enquiries and may not have their phone lines or receptions staffed; it is why you see the vast majority of charity CEO roles advertised for a lower salary than for a trainee graduate solicitor; it is why investment in charity staff training and development is so appallingly low, and it is why you so often see part-time CEOs and part-time accountants roles in the charity jobs pages. It is also one of the reasons behind the erosion of charity reserves. The Covid-19 pandemic and reduction of fundraising income in 2020 has brought to light the fact that so many charities are running on empty.

Running On Empty

A charity's reserves are the organisation's rainy-day fund and its investment pot. Organisations like charities, with highly uncertain funding arrangements, need to ensure they can fund their obligations (rent payments, redundancy costs etc.) should they suffer a catastrophic loss of funding. As funding dropped following the 2010 coalition government cuts, charities' lack of cash reserves was suddenly exposed, a situation which, sadly, we should expect to see once again as a result of Covid-19. Post-2010 a slew of charities began to founder, while many were smaller charities operating outside of the public eye, one of these casualties was a larger and better known charity. The popular 37-year old adoption and fostering network, BAAF, was not carrying forward the level of reserves it needed, it also had huge pension liabilities, and was rescued at the eleventh hour by Coram group in 2015 (Community Care 2015).

Trustees are responsible for setting out the level of reserves they want to see for their organisation. There is no formula for calculating an acceptable level of reserves. Each charity is instead expected to decide on this for themselves, taking into account the level of risk they perceive in their income streams, the amount of funding they require should they lose core incomes streams, and the amount of cash they need as working capital. In reality a commonly accepted target for charities has evolved, set at between three to six months' operating costs. The reasons for coalescing around a standard target are in themselves interesting to consider. Perhaps trustees struggle to assess the three areas above, perhaps they lack the financial skills and understanding of risk that would enable them to calculate a sensible reserves level, or perhaps they are simply reacting to indications from funders that these are 'acceptable' reserve levels.

The views which funders have about reserves can be significant for trustees. Funders will be reluctant to fund charities which hold reserves that are seen as being either too high or too low, instead they require charities to operate at a level of liquidity that is balanced between the two (which is commonly assumed to be six months' operating costs). However, while every funder expects a charity to have healthy reserves, few of them actually want to help a charity to reach a target reserves level by, for example, providing any funding over and above the running costs of a service. As the former Chair of the Charity Commission, William Shawcross, himself put it: a responsible approach to reserves "is a problem for all charities".

> We advise charities that they should spend their money, and at the same time they must have adequate reserves, so it is quite a hard act for them to follow.
> *(House of Commons 2016: 10)*

In order to increase their reserves, charities need to make a surplus in their precious unrestricted funding in the financial year, even after they have taken out the cost of their support functions.[1] Generating this surplus income is a big challenge for many charities. Equally, for those charities that happen to have reserves above the standard target level (for example those that carry high reserves due to particularly risky income streams or because they are planning a significant investment) funders can be unwilling to offer additional funding. I had this experience myself as CEO, where reserves built up to invest in the charity's development were perceived by a funder as evidence that the charity no longer needed their financial support and ought instead to 'live off' its reserves first before seeking further revenue funding.

The impact of running down reserves is two-fold: charities have no fat to help them survive lean times, as we saw in the anguished cries for help from across the sector as a result of the halt to fundraising events imposed by Covid-19 (Never More Needed 2020). If a charity loses a grant, they may need funding to keep a service going for 6 to 12 months in order to bring in new funding, or to re-develop their services. Small and mid-sized charities often lack the reserves to manage these funding gaps, the result being that they may have to make experienced staff redundant when one project ends, only to have to recruit and train new staff if future funding is secured a month or so later, because they don't have the reserve cash to bridge between projects.

The second major impact of low reserves is that charities lack the working capital to fund the research, experimentation and the development of new projects. One CEO I spoke to desperately wanted to carve out time for her staff team to spend time away from delivery to think about and develop new responses to the needs of the families they worked with, but the charity just never had the money to take staff away from their day jobs. Everything ran on a shoestring, there was no slack and all the team's energy was taken up with delivery, delivery, delivery (Interviewee T 2020). Without the freedom to experiment, to sometimes fail but always to learn, charities are severely restricted in their ability to develop new and effective responses to the issues their beneficiaries face.

Grants Musical Chairs

Not only can grant funding be restricted to a specific project; its timings are also usually restricted too. Almost all grant-makers limit the amount of time that any charity can hold a grant from them. Standard times will vary, with some grants lasting just one year or six months, where others will run for up to three years. After that grant period there is usually an enforced break where the charity cannot re-apply to that funder for a set period of time. Although there are some occasional counter-examples, securing grant funding for longer than three years is still fairly unusual (Unwin 2004:5).

The short-term nature of this funding has a big impact. More than a year in advance of any grant ending charities will need to start again on their dance to secure new funding. Crucially, they will start to do this before they have any final results from the existing project, so new applications will tend to be for a continuation of the existing project, without being able to incorporate much new learning. Thoughtful grant makers know this, and they don't like it. Former Charity Commissioner and former CEO of the Joseph Rowntree Foundation, Julia Unwin, called this 'the grant-making tango' (Unwin 2004). This constant pressure means that much of charities' energy is spent in the wrong way: on grant applications, and far less time is focused on evaluating what works and on developing new, more effective, interventions (Unwin 2004: 34).

But grant-makers persist with short term funding because they are fearful of creating dependency or 'silting up' their grant-making (Unwin 2004: 22). They don't want to be either the sole funder of a charity or its long-term funder because they fear that if they do ever withdraw funding the charity will then be unsustainable. They are also aware that there are many, many charities out there and want to be able to spread their money around as far as they can.

Dirty Money?

One potential source of cash that charities consider securing is corporate funding. Some large businesses run their own grant programmes and charity partnerships and charities explore these for potential new funding. But again, corporate partnerships and funding are not always quite the golden eggs they may seem to be. In my experience of working with many of the UK's larger companies, corporate partnerships tend to favour larger charities. There are plenty of reasons for this. One is the competitive process for partnerships. It is common for companies to run a beauty contest of kinds to select a charity to work with: this process takes significant time and resource for charities and there is no guarantee of success. The process of deciding on a charity partnership can take months in itself, but the eventual partnership may only last for one year, during which the company will already be embarking on its next charity selection process.

Sometimes these partnerships are lucrative, but they do also take a lot of time and energy to manage. Not many charities are willing to speak openly about a difficult experience with corporates (for obvious reasons), but I have seen this myself many times. When I was working on a local partnership with a national charity in 2016 that charity's entire operational management team put our partnership, and much of their other work, on hold when they secured a major corporate partnership. The partnership was worth hundreds of thousands of pounds and seemed at first to be a godsend. However, core members of staff were taken away from their day-jobs in order to set up new initiatives and run activities for the corporate partnership. This significantly impeded their ability to develop other long-term work in favour of this one, limited-term partnership.

Corporate partners may ask for regular and detailed impact reports, and they frequently expect charities to arrange events and fundraising activities too, perhaps unaware of the amount of resource these require. The smaller the charity the less likely they are to push back against onerous demands. For instance, whilst writing this book I met a mid-sized charity working with vulnerable people, where the experienced operational staff team were being taken away from their frontline delivering services to organise a fundraising walk (something none of them had ever done before) for their major corporate sponsor. They had not dared to say no.

There can also be an ethical issue with the type of company a charity agrees to work with, because companies may come with baggage. In some cases the funding relationship clearly is not tenable, for example when the company concerned is inflicting a direct harm on the beneficiaries of the charity (would it be ethical for a tobacco manufacturer to sponsor a cancer charity?). Most charities would think twice before accepting funding from big tobacco or arms manufacturers or betting shops. But until recently we probably assumed it was not controversial for BP to sponsor the Royal Shakespeare Company (RSC). Not any longer. It turns out that the people who visit the RSC care about the effect that major oil companies like BP are having on the environment, and on their children's futures and they pushed the RSC to jettison BP as a sponsor (RSC undated).

Sometimes charities can make the argument that, in taking the money of corporates running the sorts of business that directly harm their beneficiaries, they are making the company pay a restitution of sorts. So a brand of betting shops may be promoting exactly the sort of addictive gambling which caused a charity's service users to get into insurmountable debt, but then the betting shops donate tens of thousands of pounds to help support those people affected. It is not forbidden for charities to take corporate funding of course and some charities, in particular charitable foundations, are associated with for-profit companies at root. However, some companies' work may bring with it such a toxic reputational blow that a cash donation just would not outweigh any damage done.

One such example is the controversial drugs company Purdue Pharma which is accused of fuelling the opioid epidemic in the US and is owned by the Sackler family (of the Sackler Trust). The Sackler Trust is a longstanding supporter of the arts, many galleries include Sackler wings for example, but the reputation of Purdue Pharma has rung alarm bells with some donation recipients, resulting in actions such as the Louvre's decision to remove the name Sackler from its galleries in 2019 (although, interestingly, other galleries have not done so at the time of writing) (Harris 2019). There are obvious reasons for such companies to want to engage in very public support for good causes as an attempt to launder their own reputations. The key point here for charities is that any reputational bonuses for the company involved are a by-product of the charity's work, not its end goal, and the charity needs to weigh up the potential harmful impact of any reputational issues against the benefits of the donation received.

But this subtlety, I believe, still leaves the public feeling uneasy. Even if charities are allowed to take this money the charity brand may seem compromised: would a debt-advice charity directly criticise the betting shops now that they have become a major funder? Isn't it tantamount to biting the hand that feeds you? Worse, hasn't the charity now got a perverse incentive to see big profits in the betting shops, made from vulnerable people, in order to see more funding come through to their charity partnership?

Fair Trade?

So, if charities' income from donors, contracts and grants comes with steel strings attached could trading provide a freer form of income? Raising money through selling services and products isn't new in the charity sector. Think of charity shops. Some charities were even formed as trading organisations: the Youth Hosteling Association (YHA) opened its doors in 1929 as a charity that charged for its accommodation, but saw its primary (charitable) purpose as a response to inadequate living conditions for Britain's urban poor, in particular for young people. The inscription on the YHA National Office in St Albans reads:

> The buildings are diverse in character but they have a common purpose: to help all, especially young people of limited means, to a greater knowledge, love and care of the countryside.

From its inception the YHA raised money through payment for its accommodation. Over the years it has supplemented this with specific grant funding but its trading has been central to its work. When James Blake took over as CEO of the YHA it was such a successful business that he noted how few people even knew that the YHA was a charity (Blake 2020).

The relationship between charities and trading can be complex. But it is also very common. We, the public, just do not tend to see it or give it much thought until it is thrust in front of our noses, usually in the form of a charity-in-money-scandal-shocker. Charities may sell products and services as long as their primary activity is charitable. This income is extremely welcome because it is unrestricted funding with fewer strings attached. However, there are strings of a different kind, which relate to the expectations of the public in relation to trading.

Companies are rewarded for trading in an ethical manner: consumers might even be willing to pay more for sustainable or ethically produced products (Whelan and

Kronthal-Sacco 2019); investors are looking for investable ethical companies to support through ESG funds, and employees increasingly want to work for ethical brands (Cone 2016). Companies are rewarded because they are seen to be doing more than they absolutely have to. They are making a conscious choice to do the right thing, so to speak. Charities on the other hand are held to a much higher level of accountability. We don't reward charities for doing the right thing, we expect them to do so.

Not only are charities expected to trade to impeccable ethical standards, they face major challenges in running successful trading arms because of the competition for skills and a clash of culture. In 2019 I chaired a conference discussion about ethical entrepreneurship in which panellists agreed that what makes for a successful trading charity are (1) the right people and (2) the right culture. Anyone who has worked across the private and charity sectors knows that the prevailing culture and skills in a charity are very different from those of a business. When a charity wants to sell a product or service it needs accomplished salespeople – experienced staff with an entrepreneurial mindset. It will often need to compete with the private sector for staff with this experience, which means it needs to be able to pay a comparable salary.

Not being able to pay competitively can mean that charities struggle to build the skilled team they need to be able to trade effectively. Even if charities do manage to recruit these staff, a charity's non-entrepreneurial culture could hamper their trading efforts, for example by holding them back from operating at pace, not meeting sales targets, or not engaging in practices which their competitors may employ (such as aggressive advertising campaigns). These obstacles can place the charity at a competitive disadvantage.

Smart charities like the YHA have found a way to make this work for them, by capitalising on their social business credentials and marketing themselves as an ethical business, which appeals to their target market. For other charities, which lack the skills and financial clout of the YHA, straddling this divide and trading successfully could seem like an insurmountable set of hurdles.

Social Investment

As the jaws of the financial crash closed around the charity sector after 2010, the government was keen to promote a new form of finance for the sector. Social investment seemed to offer a halfway house where charities' successful interventions could be funded in advance by third parties, which would then be paid back, plus interest, when the work was complete. The charity St Giles Trust was a pioneer of this with their Peterborough One Service, a wrap-around programme designed to respond to the complex needs of offenders to help them break the cycle of reoffending. It worked at its most basic level like this:

1.   17 investors paid St Giles in advance through the Peterborough Social Impact Bond to cut the re-offending rate of short-sentenced offenders leaving Peterborough prison by 7.5%.

2.   St Giles delivered a partnership of services which reduced re-offending (they achieved a 9% reduction).
3.   The Ministry of Justice paid for the successful interventions.
4.   The investors recouped their investment plus 3% interest from commissioner's payment. *(Owen 2017)*

Sounds simple. In fact, taking up social investment seems anathema to many charities, according to financial sustainability and social investment, expert Mark Salway. Rather than this being a simple question of technical understanding, Salway identifies a deeper, cultural mindset required for social investment which charities tend to lack:

> The charity sector often lacks a long-term investment mindset – this includes the use of social investment. As a result, charity trustees don't understand the investment needed to create new opportunities, or invest in infrastructure for the future.

This stands in marked contrast to the social enterprise sector, which Salway characterises as being far more entrepreneurial and investment-minded in general. Where charities struggle with growing their revenue models and even costing their interventions effectively, how can they manage social investment effectively, he argues (Salway 2020).

A similar challenge arose with the attempted introduction of payment-by-results (PbR) by commissioners. This operates in a similar way to social investment, although it can be at a smaller scale. The main difference is that the charity is not able to access working capital in the form of a loan, but must deliver its contract first and risk not being paid if it fails to deliver on any of the pre-agreed outcomes. The PbR system and its impact on charities has been analysed in great detail by NCVO. They set out the host of challenges this presents to charities, not least the need to develop or hire wholly new skills and to have sufficient reserves to manage the cash flow and the risk involved (Sheil and Breidenbach-Rose 2014: 12, 4).

Funding Forecast

Charities are beset by a range of different funding challenges which larger organisations are best placed to navigate, while smaller ones are under most pressure to diversify. The effort that goes into securing and then servicing these funding pots takes up all the available oxygen of smaller to mid-sized charities. So, what does this mean for the way that charities meet the challenges of the coming decades?

Firstly, there is the matter of working capital, or lack thereof. It is common for charities to be working 'right down to the metal' as one of my former trustees liked to say. With dwindling reserves and restricted funding, charities lack the slack in their finances that make planning and innovation possible. Charities running on empty have no time to horizon scan, to evaluate, to think and to listen. Nor do they have time to risk failure by trialling new services. All of these elements are essential to innovation.

A lack of working capital reduces a charity's ability to collaborate as there is limited time to develop relationships that may lead to partnerships. The competition for funding also pits charities against one another, so they tend to develop a defensive and inward-looking mindset. This lack of collaboration further weakens charities' ability to develop new and improved support for the cause they have been created to tackle, not only because of the likelihood of duplication but also because it limits learning. For instance, one charity in Swansea may have run a back-to-work service which they find has some fundamental flaws, but they don't share their findings. A similar charity in Nottingham then goes on to set up an identical service and it fails all over again. Had the two put their heads together they could have developed a much-improved service, learning from the failings of the first iteration and resulting in many more people getting into decent jobs. But this rarely happens in the charity sector, unless it is forced upon the charities by a funder.

Similarly, a small charity may have developed an effective way of supporting young carers into higher education, but it does not have the reach or expertise to scale-up this project. When it comes to the end of its three-year funding its evaluation report is filed on the shelf of a funder and the project closes. No similar charities get to hear about the elements which made it successful and there is no blueprint to enable them to replicate the service, so many thousands of young carers lose out on this support. This waste of knowledge was mentioned to me over and again by leaders from across the sector who see the need to share learning to improve services, but are frustrated by the incentives pushing them in the wrong direction.

The complex way in which charities work means that a huge amount of work is involved in just securing enough money to keep going. This is a major barrier to charities being able to plan for the future. As Sir Harvey McGrath outlined to me:

> Short term funding cycles leading to cliff edges. [As a result] the CEO's focus is on fundraising, with less time to spend planning for the future. This results in a focus on survival, not growth and development.
>
> (McGrath 2020)

A more insidious challenge for charities arises from their increasingly diverse sources of funding, and the uncertainty that this leads to in the public's imagination. Many people feel that charities have moved from being a clear-cut (if mythical) form of organisation that they felt they understood, to a weird hybrid doing whatever it takes, however dubious, in order to survive. Unfortunately, this uncertainty both leads to, and is the product of, a vicious circle: the less the public trusts a charity the less money is donated, this pushes the charity to seek new income generation options, like trading. This in turns gradually undermines public sense of trust and certainty about what charities are for and how they differ from businesses (Figure 4.1).

Looking ahead, this situation seems unsustainable. Charities should be aware of the trend towards a radical transparency, which is just emerging in fundraising and

Less money is donated and/or donations are restricted

Charity seeks new funding sources

Charity diversifies funding (trading, public sector contracts etc)

Public doubts about where money goes in new 'hybrid' charities

Charity spends more on fundraising to sustain new sources

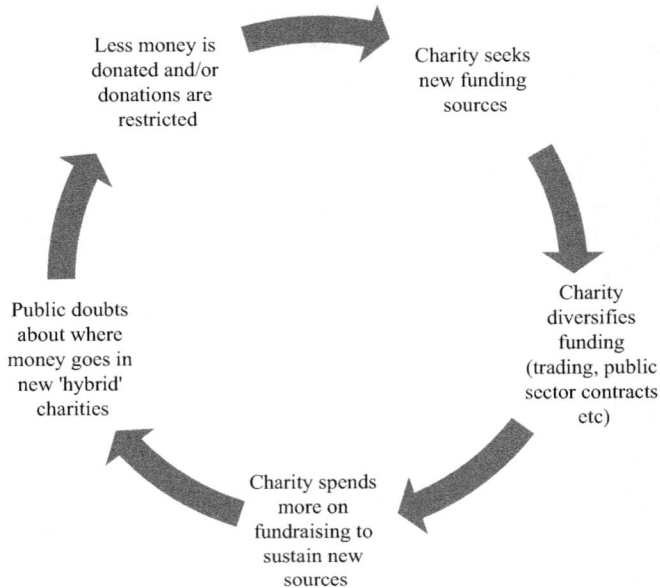

FIGURE 4.1 The ever-decreasing circle of charity funding diversification and public trust

which they should expect to see cutting through to donors' expectations about charity funding. It will no longer be enough to report that 'xx% of your donations go direct to our projects': it will not be acceptable to continue the fiction of low 'overheads'. Instead, charities will need to have an honest conversation with their donors about what it costs to run a professional organisation and the level and length of funding that is needed to deliver meaningful, measurable and high-quality services.

There are some interesting examples emerging, from Save the Children's decision to publish the salaries and benefits of each of their senior directors in their annual report, to Clic Sargent's impact report, which listed failures alongside successes, and the Charity Defense Council's campaigns in the US to tackle the myth of the 'overhead' (Clic Sargent 2019). Charities of the future will need to adopt a different way of raising funding and a more open way of engaging with the public on how they spend their income and why. Achieving this though will require a radical change in culture for many UK charities.

Note

1   This surplus is only useful if it relates to unrestricted funding, restricted funding when underspent simply accumulates, as we have seen, in a locked part of the reserves, which the charity can't access, even in an emergency.

5

HOW SHOULD CHARITIES BE MANAGED?

CASE STUDY: RSPCA

In October 2018 a survey by the trade union Unite revealed that 3 in 10 staff at the major animal charity RSPCA reported that they had been bullied. 46% of staff felt that bullying was a problem within the culture at the charity and an astonishing 90% of those surveyed had experienced at least one 'negative behaviour' in the last year, which included unmanageable workloads, having their opinions ignored, being given unreasonable deadlines, or being required to do work below their level of competence (Kay 2018). Despite leadership promises, one year later *Charity Times* reported similar numbers in a follow-up survey in the summer of 2019 (Weymouth 2019). This was compounded by the charity's decision to introduce new contracts which included some element of performance-related pay measures, which Unite said could "exacerbate plummeting staff morale in an organisation where bullying has been endemic and not dealt with effectively" (ibid). As a result the charity hit the headlines again with more than 70% of staff voting for strike action in February 2020. This was an eye-opening insight into workplace culture and conflict at the heart of one of the nation's best-loved and long-standing large charities.

In recent years the way that charities are run, as much as the work that they do, has been under the spotlight. The wider press has circled around the question of charity leaders' pay, and the charity press and charities themselves have spent much time and energy focused on the way that charities treat their staff, with issues of bullying, mental health at work and diversity making headlines most weeks in 2019.

DOI: 10.4324/9781003139089-5

Registered charities, which are often also limited companies, are required to operate under most of the same regulations which govern private companies. As employers they are subject to the same laws and they do not have any special restrictions on, for example, salaries. However, public expectations, and charities' own expectations, about the way in which they should operate are much higher than for other organisations. Charities are berated, and berate themselves, for instances of staff bullying (Fitzpatrick and Thorne 2019), for burn-out and pressure causing stress (Kay 2019), for a lack of ethnic diversity in senior roles (ACEVO 2018), for employing too many CEOs who studied at Oxford or Cambridge (Whitehead 2019), for paying staff too much (Keogh and Braithwaite 2019), for paying staff too little (Living Wage Foundation 2017), for having too few disabled people in charity roles (Cooney 2019), and for having trustee boards with too little diversity (Charity Commission et al. 2017).

Things are different in the private sector. While scrutiny of private companies over diversity, the gender pay gap and mental health has increased in recent years, in my view the level of expectations, and the ability to meet these expectations, in private companies is very different from those in charities. It is only occasionally that specific businesses or industries make headlines on issues of poor management or bullying, such as the insurance industry's problem with sexism and alcohol (BBC 2019). Oxbridge degrees amongst private sector or public sector leaders are not newsworthy, companies' payment of below-survival level wages only makes the news occasionally, and the lack of diversity in business is only news when the gender pay-gap gets reported or when Black Lives Matter managed to cut through to public consciousness in 2020.

The focus of press criticism on the ways in which charities operate underlines two things: that the public has very high expectations of charities as employers and organisations; and that charities are subject to a whole host of unwritten rules about how they go about their work, which do not apply to the same degree to for-profit, private sector, organisations. The public has an unspoken assumption that charities are or should be more compassionate, kinder, less target-driven places to work than companies. But many aspects of working in this way have a cost in both money and in time, both of which are scarce commodities in the charity sector. This then provokes some important questions about where charities focus their resources: should charities invest in the way they run their organisation? If so, how much? And does this take investment away from their charitable cause?

In my experience charities take issues such as diversity, bullying and fair pay extremely seriously and are highly motivated to eradicate these harmful practices. But the high expectations (often unspoken) placed on charities, both by charities themselves and by other stakeholders, do also influence the way in which charities operate and the focus of their attention. The constant pressure to meet these expectations stretches charities' attention and resources, and impacts it their ability to change and respond to the evolving world around them.

Also, just because the people in a charity are delivering a caring and compassionate service, we can't assume that the management culture is, and should be, caring and compassionate without limits. Of course, most charities aspire to be great employers running the most efficient operations, but achieving this is more challenging for charities than it is for ordinary for-profit businesses. Charities' decisions about how they operate will always involve some level of ethical trade-off, balancing the best possible practice against their available resources and their charitable mission.

Nice People Doing Good Things

Working in a charity is a job just like any other. If you're employed by a charity, you have just the same rights as your friend who works for a bank. And your employer, whether it's the RNLI, your local Age UK branch or local super-market, has the same responsibilities as any other employer. A friend of mine who works in TV, on meeting my charity sector friends, commented on how much nicer they were than 'media people'. It is true that many of us who work in the sector are decent people, but then so are many of the people I know who work in businesses. And I am sorry to reveal that I have come across a number of difficult and unpleasant people in the charity sector, as in any other sector.

The people who work in charities vary as much as in other sectors, and the ways charities are run vary enormously also. As recent stories about safeguarding, bullying and mental health in Oxfam, Save the Children and the RSPCA have revealed, just because a charity is pursuing an important cause and caring for its beneficiaries, it doesn't necessarily follow that it is run flawlessly (Wallis 2019). In today's world though it is not enough for a charity to do good work, the way in which it delivers that work is also under scrutiny. As Karl Wilding, then Director of Policy at NCVO, put it in the House of Lords Select Committee on Charities:

> Charities are no different from all other institutions, in that they face a greater level of scrutiny over how they work. The fact that they do good in and of itself is no longer good enough. How they do that good is something that people are increasingly asking questions about.
>
> *(House of Lords 2017: 68)*

I would go further than this and argue that charities face a far higher degree of scrutiny than the companies I have worked with. They face higher expectations about the way that they work, and that scrutiny comes from within the sector as well as from outside. As Vicky Browning (ACEVO) and Sarah Hughes (Centre for Mental Health) put it in their introduction to a report specifically about bullying in charities:

> Bullying can happen in any workplace but we believe that civil society should be taking the lead on tackling workplace bullying and creating inclusive and supportive cultures. As well as being positive for staff and volunteers, inclusive cultures that have a focus on well-being are more productive and innovative, so

taking action is good for our workers, our volunteers, our organisations and most importantly the people and causes we serve.

(Fitzpatrick and Thorne 2019: 5)

Charities, then, should not just be doing the right thing: they are expected, even by those within the sector, to be paragons. This is a view that seems to be shared by the wider public. We have seen a strong public reaction against charities running direct marketing campaigns with powerful, emotive content, even though these tactics are regularly employed by for-profit companies. The public and donors react negatively to charities paying their staff more competitive salaries. Public expectations of charities are high and, in addition, contradictory demands are being placed on charities by their huge and shifting range of stakeholders.

Too Many Cooks

Charities have many different stakeholders: trustees, beneficiaries, volunteers, employees, funders and donors all expect a charity to operate in different ways. Sometimes these expectations overlap, but often they are contradictory. A funder may push a charity to develop new business to generate income from trading, which requires a more businesslike approach, but volunteers drift away from a charity that feels too businesslike, where staff do not have time to chat and volunteers are set specific, time-bound tasks.

Commissioners and funders expect a charity to have some basic aspects of business management in place, such as specific training for work with vulnerable people, databases for reporting, reliable IT infrastructure and clear lines of responsibility for delivery. They often require evidence that all of these things are in place before awarding a contract, and that safeguarding for vulnerable people ensures that volunteers' support roles are limited. The same charity's individual donors however, may be dismayed to find that their donations could be used to pay for a database, or that volunteers are no longer able to deliver support.

Even the expectations of one single stakeholder can be contradictory. For example, a funder will expect a charity to run a high quality, efficient and effective service, but may refuse to pay for the true ('overhead' or 'admin') costs of delivering these services – which include management, infrastructure, IT network, specialist staff and training. One charity CEO told me about a single charitable trust with contradictory expectations about their charity's plan to professionalise:

> Despite wanting us to diversify our funding to become more sustainable, some trusts and foundations express concern that [our charity] is too ambitious and 'too worried about the bottom line'. For example, one funder paid for [an impact consultancy] to help the charity to scale, but then seemed unhappy to see us go ahead with the recommendations. They were

uncomfortable about our plans for growth, even though that's what they
wanted us to do, to scale, in the first place.

(Interviewee U 2020).

Charities have to balance these conflicting expectations daily, often by re-pre-
senting what they do in different ways to the different audiences, and by playing
down or emphasising different aspects of their work in line with the expectations
of each of their stakeholders.

In Praise of Management

A well-managed organisation is a more efficient organisation, which is more likely to
deliver more effective services. We know this from business management 101: not even
the leanest tech firm does without management structures. Many of the basic employee
issues such as bullying, grievances, poor staff retention and stress can be avoided or
minimised through good management. In my role at Heart of the City, advising businesses on how to operate with a strong social purpose, I was regularly struck by how
much of being a responsible business relied on something as simple as the basics of good,
effective management. Charities working with vulnerable people need good managers
to prevent staff burnout, to support caseloads and run a safe service.

As charities grow beyond a dozen employees some formal management structure is needed, but the funding of management roles and management training is
too often seen by grant-makers or donors as 'bureaucracy' or 'overheads' rather
than an integral part of the service that it truly is. Instead funders like to see
charities demonstrating frugality, a mindset which is actively unhelpful because it
causes charities to under-invest in their core infrastructure, which can be termed
'overhead', i.e. in research and development, IT, marketing and vital training.
Gregory Dees argues that this 'emphasis on sacrifice', which I recognise from my
own experience in the sector, drives charities to focus on the meaningless performance measure of the ratio of overheads costs to overall expenditure. This is at
the expense of understanding and improving the charity's impact, or even its cost
effectiveness in achieving this impact (Dees 2012).

Funders' reluctance to pay for the full cost of delivering the work they want to
support means that the costs of management often need to be found from a
charity's precious pool of unrestricted income. As we have seen, there is already a
significant call on this type of income, and the question for charities is how much
should they spend on *how* they run their organisation as opposed to delivering
their core mission. Bluntly, how much can they afford to spend? Or, more per-
tinently, can they afford not to do this? As Clara Miller puts it:

The truth is, not only is it difficult to afford the management improvements
that must accompany growth, it is difficult even to afford the ongoing
improvements necessary to maintain effective and efficient operations *without*

growth. As a result, management (as opposed to program) is frequently staffed too thinly and under-supported in relationship to program .... The irony is that a technique meant to control costs and focus efforts on mission actually undermines efficiency and harms program.

(Miller 2003: 7)

So, charities need to invest in management and infrastructure in order to stay still as well as to grow. This investment is in fact crucial to the successful development of other 'frontline' (or, as Miller describes it, "program") work. But running a charity on a shoestring and with restricted project funding means that this sort of investment is not often possible. For instance, if a charity is unable to pay for enough managers, staff working on emotionally wearing caseloads may go without any chance to de-brief, which takes its toll over time and may result in stress or burnout. Similarly, if the charity cannot afford to pay a competitive wage, good staff will leave on a regular basis and the whole team is put under more pressure. Of course, any CEO would want to employ the right ratio of managers to workers, and all of us would prefer to pay at least the real living wage. But a charity CEO's options to pay for extra staff and higher salaries are very limited.

Ethical Workplace

One charity CEO told me:

I know that I am not paying my staff a high enough pension. What they get here won't be enough for them to live on when they retire. They work so hard. I would love to be able to offer them something above the statutory minimum employer contribution but where would I get the money?

(Interviewee T 2020)

This CEO had already reduced her own working hours and salary to make ends meet. Another former charity CEO expressed his frustration about inadequate pay for parental leave:

It is a scandal that many charities don't pay more than SMT [statutory maternity pay] but they just can't afford it and funders don't [cover] this.

(Pomroy 2020)

I have experienced this challenge myself. At Heart of the City, staff were employed on local authority contracts with generous parental leave benefits but the charity didn't receive extra grant funding to cover these costs. This meant that whenever a member of staff took parental leave the charity had to either pay for the equivalent of two posts for a nine-month period, or leave the post vacant and put the work on ice. We were fortunate enough to have built up sufficient reserves to cover this eventuality, but many charities are not in this position. Similarly, charities may wish to provide all staff with a cost of living salary increase each year, reflecting the fact that inflation erodes static pay levels year on year. However, grant settlements from funders rarely allow for these increases. As a result, charities who do make this commitment to their staff will find themselves having to make up the difference between salaries payable and salaries funded from their precious unrestricted income or from reserves.

The fact is that charities cannot easily afford to be paragons of ethical management, much as they might want to be. Charities' money and their energies are finite and so when a charity prioritises parental leave or salary uplifts, there is a risk that its other stakeholders may question whether the charity is too focused on its staff at the expense of its beneficiaries. In reality charities have to make ethical trade-offs, they have to decide which issues matter most to them, and which are most in line with their mission.

To give an example, if a small mental health charity wanted to set an example by chiefly employing staff who themselves had mental health conditions this would be a powerful example of a charity living its values. However, the charity's funders would be unlikely to cover the cost of long-term sick leave. As a result then, if this charity did have a significant number of team members who, due to their own significant health conditions, were regularly off work for long periods of time, the charity would not be able to pay for cover. This could risk advice lines not being covered and projects running behind time, effecting the reliability of the service and with very real impacts on their beneficiaries. This is not to say that such a charity would be wrong to employ potential service users and to support them, far from it, but it is important to recognise that sometimes a choice has to be made in organisations with limited resources about where that resource is focused and how much attention and money they can afford to spend on running the ideal organisation.

A Professional Culture

Charities are under pressure to diversify their income so that they are not too dependent on a single source, which may not last. But diversifying income brings new challenges and growth requires infrastructure, as Miller points out (Miller 2003: 7). Being more structured brings with it more responsibilities, from managing paid staff, to accounting for increasingly complex finances, to taking on grants or contracts which the charity must then deliver and report back on. These factors push charities to become more professional, to achieve greater efficiency and to be more strategic.

Leaders in the charity sector regularly bemoan the fact that charities are being asked to operate more and more like private companies: they are asked to find efficiencies (the dreaded mantra of 'more for less'), to be responsive to their 'customers', to generate income from a range of sources, and to deliver professional levels of service to vulnerable people. Charities commonly emphasise the cultural difference between themselves and businesses, as relying on trust and communal accountability rather than market relationships (Hyndman 2017). As the pressure to professionalise increases, this can provoke questions around the purpose of a charity, a tension which has been present in discussion about charities for a long time (Smith 2019): on the one hand charities remain full of people with a passion for the cause and they do still rely on 'trust relationships', on the other hand charities are increasingly engaged in delivering highly professional work involving 'contractual accountability', and which requires specialist skills and training.

When I started work in the charity sector, in homelessness charities, many of the people I worked with had many years' experience supporting homeless people on the streets and in hostels. They had helped to deliver the government's Rough Sleepers' Initiative, which had almost eradicated street homelessness in the UK, they had lived and breathed this work for 20 years and would not have considered working in another area. When I resigned from Shelter in 2008, I remember my then-manager looking at me in astonishment, 'I thought you were a Shelter person?' she said.

This sort of identification with an organisation and/or a cause generates the level of motivation that many private sector firms can only dream of. Still, it has its risks. It can cause workers to feel frustrated by the development of more transactional relationships, in which they are held to account in a more professional way. Passion for a cause is essential in some community-based and volunteer-run charities, such as local sports clubs. It is this strong sense of purpose that motivates the volunteers who run the services to turn up and deliver childrens' activities or community support work. However, when charities grow, this emotional commitment amongst volunteers and staff can morph into a drag on innovation and an unwillingness to change, as we shall see.

Beyond charity employees and amongst the wider public an uneasiness about this process of charity professionalisation remains. This attitude is not new, indeed it was recognised by the predecessor to the National Council for Voluntary Organisations (NCVO) as early as 1984:

> The Council confronted the accusation that the sector's increased professionalism somehow implied a loss of values: 'Many voluntary organisations', it argued, 'are engaged in sophisticated work and require a high level of managerial, organizational and professional skills like other modern organisations.' Any suggestion that the involvement of paid staff and a commitment to effectiveness undermined the 'true character' of voluntary groups was dismissed as 'anachronistic'.
>
> *(Smith 2019: 174)*

As charities grow, they change: they employ (more) staff and employing staff means meeting basic employment conditions, having the correct insurance in place and HR advice. Delivering services set out in grants and contracts results in charities having to record the results or impact of their work. The larger the charity, the more complex its internal systems become. A very small team of volunteers, where no transfer of intelligence about service users is required, is very different from a charity with 16 paid staff members, who all need to share information about the people they are all supporting, whilst keeping this secure, to comply with data protection regulations. Running an operation of this nature will mean that a charity needs to invest in a secure database and that staff need to be trained on how to use this. Similarly a larger team requires some line management, so funding has to be found for people who are not spending their entire time working directly with beneficiaries. Some staff will need to be employed to manage and support others, while others will be needed to look after the technology, including the database; a trained accountant will need to manage the finances, and so on.

Obviously each charity is different, but even the most lean and efficient organisation cannot afford not to invest in some level of infrastructure in order to deliver effective services. Sophisticated organisations need sophisticated structures and some specialist skills, and this work cannot be done on passion alone: it requires solid experience of organisational management. Again, this prevailing culture of sacrifice works against charities:

> Solving social problems is difficult work, requiring skills comparable to, perhaps even greater than, those in demand in the business world. Searching for people willing and able to accept modest or low salaries imposes costs on social entrepreneurs, as does the turnover when people leave because their families and financial needs have grown, and they can no longer afford to stay with the organization. This is one of the barriers to scaling effective social innovations— the difficulty of attracting and retaining sufficient affordable and skilled talent.
>
> *(Dees 2012)*

Social Entrepreneurs or Aid Workers?

As we have seen, there is a split in charities between those that are engaged in the 'modern culture of problem-solving' and those focused on 'alms-giving' (Dees 2012). These two aims of alms-giving and problem-solving, serve very different purposes, and the two can be at odds. Alms-giving speaks to a subjective, instinctive urge to altruism, which is challenging to channel and to direct (MacAskill 2015). Problem-solving on the other hand takes a much more objective view of how a charity should be run and what ought to be prioritised, and is neatly summarised by William MacAskill

> It costs about $50,000 to train and provide one guide dog for one blind person, something that would significantly improve that person's quality of life. However, if we could use that $50,000 to completely cure someone of blindness, that would be an even better use of money since it provides a larger benefit for the same cost.
>
> *(MacAskill 2015)*

This clash of values between giving relief and solving underlying problems is one of the most challenging aspects of running a charity. Different stakeholders can expect a single organisation to be both of these things. And when charities attempt to behave differently, in a way which challenges donors, employees or volunteers' expectations, this can impinge on their values, provoking strong reactions.

Stakeholders' instincts for charities to economise, to cut costs, to run a service on the absolute minimum, are embedded in the culture of the sector and in the minds of many of those who fund its work. But underinvestment in a charity's infrastructure and staff skills also limits its ability to achieve impact at scale, and therefore to solve the problems it is founded, and funded, to tackle. As Dees puts it:

> The culture of charity views sacrifice as a means of demonstrating that your caritas (charity) is genuine. This has resulted in pressure for misguided frugality that can undermine serious problem-solving efforts. While pressure to economize is generally a good thing, this norm has inhibited investments in valuable capacity building and made it difficult to attract and retain problem-solving talent.
>
> *(Dees 2012)*

This culture of sacrifice lies at the heart of many of the problems that charities face in moving into the modern world. Charities are under pressure to justify everything they do, which is not a 'sacrifice' – a decent salary, decent pension, reasonable working hours, basic management and working IT. These are the things which private companies have much more agency over, in their operations. While this hairshirt approach may have worked for alms-giving, small charities, it is just not appropriate for charities genuinely seeking to tackle major social issues in the 2020s.

Ethical Entrepreneurship

In 2017/18 charities earned a total of 47% or £25.3bn of funding from competitively commissioned contracts and from income generation (NCVO 2020). In the field of commissioned contracts (and also in some areas of trading) charities are often in direct competition with private sector companies and, in order to secure and then to deliver these contracts, charities have had to take on some of the characteristics of for-profit companies. These characteristics include a more target-focused type of management style, with an emphasis on measurable outputs and key performance indicators (KPIs), and a more transactional relationship with staff and volunteers. For a period of time this led some charities to over-value leaders from the private sector, and in the early 2010s, trustee boards were keen to secure those with private-sector experience to lead major charities, bringing with them a more corporate culture (Gatenby Sanderson undated).

To some extent this was an inevitable consequence of taking on competitive public contracting. Charities had to demonstrate their effectiveness and cost-effectiveness in comparison to private sector players. But this does also bring with it a conflict with their founding values and the general public's understanding of charities. As Hyndman puts it:

> [Charities'] strength comes from the value society places on the social capital that they generate, and the trust and confidence that society has in them and their employees.
>
> *(Hyndman 2017)*

So, the more that charities operate like businesses, the more they are at odds with the way in which the wider public expects them to operate. This risks undermining charities' legitimacy in the eyes of the public: if some charities behave like for-profit companies, then the public may start to perceive all charities in the way they do companies – with less trust – resulting in fewer donations and less volunteering.

The Youth Hostelling Association, a social enterprise since its inception, is an organisation that has grappled with this cultural conflict throughout its history. Current CEO, James Blake, described to me the organisation's oscillation between charity and business cultures.

CASE STUDY: YHA

When James Blake joined the YHA the charity was enjoying unprecedented success, with high levels of bookings and a healthy turnover and surplus. However, a significant number of staff and members did not realise that the YHA was a charity. It felt as though the charity was at risk of losing sight of what it was doing it all for.

After all, the YHA had been founded as a social business, with all its profits intended to be ploughed back into its mission. Although it has always charged for its hostels, it has always done so with a charitable mission at its heart.

Blake recognised that this meant they were missing out on a vital part of their identity as a social business with a unique heritage and mission. He set about re-affirming the charity's mission and how it delivered this. Now, in any YHA hostel you can see messages about its history all around. The organisation has also invested more significantly in fundraising for projects to enable disadvantaged young people to access activities and the countryside. This has been instrumental in shifting the organisation's culture and brand, and attracting staff, volunteers and customers for whom the YHA's social purpose really resonates.

There was a need to find a common language across staff doing 'social purpose' work and those doing business roles, and a need to constantly balance the charity and business focus. Blake notes that the weighting to belief, passion and emotion amongst employees and members can make it difficult to reach a compromise or agreement because it impinges on individuals' values. This makes it difficult to meld cultures because it is difficult to find ways to understand different perspectives.

However, this has meant juggling two cultures. The organisation's commercial success derived from a decade of hiring from the private sector, drawing on the experience of those in the hospitality industry to run an efficient and competitive operation. Shifting the mindset to operate in a social business is a big challenge.

(Blake 2020)

James Blake identifies a major challenge for charities aiming to diversify their income. Running an effective business requires the sorts of skills and mindset which the charity sector does not furnish its staff with. In researching this book I spoke in some depth to a successful tech entrepreneur who is now working with charities to develop and incubate tech solutions to social challenges. He mentioned to me how surprised he was that some of the basic business management and business development tools were completely unknown to charity leaders. This echoes the views of many of those I have interviewed, that many of the individuals leading charities actually have very little exposure to other sectors.

In small to mid-sized charities, employees and managers have rarely worked in the private sector and few have professional-level business training. This has a significant impact on the way they run their organisations, with a limited range of examples and experience to draw on. Others I interviewed described the charity sector as a bubble and 'insular':

Charities assume that businesses are bad, so they get stuck in an echo chamber. They need the challenge of other viewpoints.

(Interviewee S 2020)

In my experience there can be a sense of exceptionalism in the charity sector, a sense that the sector is different (and better) than other sectors. There is also, after years of having New Public Management styles of working thrust upon charities, a resentment of businesses assuming that their ways of working can be simply grafted onto charity culture. I understand this frustration, but I do also believe that there are interesting and useful experiences, which charity leaders can learn from the private sector. As one CEO put it to me "We could learn so much from business, while still retaining the culture of charity" (Interviewee V 2020). Without strong business training, exposure to other ways of working, and a more entrepreneurial mindset, it is small wonder that charity leaders find it challenging to think about and plan for the sector's future development.

R&D and Competition

Few charities have their own research and development (R&D) function, in fact I expect that very few even consider spending precious unrestricted income or reserves on setting this up. If charities were businesses, investors would steer clear of any which did not invest in R&D. After all, how could a business be prepared for future markets and changing customers without its own research and development? Failing to develop the next generation of products and services is viewed as short term and a dead-end in business, but in charities we accept it as the norm.

Not all piloted projects in the development phase succeed. In the business world venture capitalists invest in promising companies with a sanguine acceptance that around 50% will fail, but knowing that just one successful project will yield a significant return on their investment. Charities do not share this mindset, nor, crucially, do many of their funders (with rare exceptions, such as the investment-focused funder Impetus-PEF). Developing new services and testing interventions before rolling them out pays off in the long run, as services will be more relevant and more impactful. But charities, unlike businesses, are not used to taking on business risk, and without the backing of a supportive and patient funder they are likely to lack the working capital to do this.

Companies do not invest in researching and developing new products and services simply for the joy of innovation. As Banerjee and Duflo put it: "firms innovate less out of a desire for knowledge than to make sure they get there before the competition" (Banerjee and Duflo 2019). Companies are forced to innovate because they know that their marketplace is constantly on the move. If they do not change there are obvious incentives for new entrants to muscle in and win over some of their customers.

This has happened recently in financial services, an area I am familiar with from my role at Heart of the City. So-called 'challenger banks' such as Starling and Monzo offered customers something different, such as the chance to sign-up for accounts online without the bureaucracy of traditional bank applications. Some 'challengers' offered low transaction fees for foreign currency transactions and they developed a more user-friendly interface which enabled them to lure younger and tech-savvy customers away from traditional banks. They also, incidentally, attracted employees away from old-fashioned banks to work in their shared workspaces with beer and yoga onsite.

Although these new companies have relatively small market share compared with familiar high street banks (and have subsequently encountered difficulties with growth), one significant result of their development has been that the traditional banks have had to change their own services to keep up with increased customer expectations. This was true disruption in action, pushing banks to rush to find new, more attractive offers. Nothing like this has happened in the charity sector, despite the fact that many commentators expected disruption would follow on naturally from the dramatic changes to the funding landscape over the last ten years. The assumption was that charities would be left with less money and a new operating environment, in which they would need to innovate, and at pace. How can it be that after the loss of so much grant income the sector at the very top and the very bottom seems, cosmetically at least, largely unchanged from 2010?

A lot of this has to do with the culture of charities, which in turn stems from their funding and stakeholder relationships. When charity income decreased post 2010, instead of a brimming up of innovation we saw charities double down, intent on cutting costs and surviving. Instead of imaginatively re-engineering services, existing charities asked staff to take pay cuts, or reduce their hours. Reduced income is not an aid to innovation, as Charles Handy has set out: "When income, productivity or reputation is falling it is hard to contemplate anything new" (Smith 2019: 278).

Unlike businesses, super-major charities are not often worried about challengers because newcomers have been effectively priced out of high-yield fundraising, as we have seen. In the business world large companies are not the best innovators but the difference is that they see the need for innovation, so as not to be eclipsed by start-ups. Large companies routinely buy in this innovation by acquiring the start-ups. We have seen this happen frequently in Silicon Valley, where tech giants buy up and absorb promising start-ups, for example Google parent company Alphabet is reputed to have spent tens of billions of dollars acquiring as many as 200 companies (Reynolds 2017). These acquisitions effectively purchased innovation, as well as draining competition.

Things couldn't be more different in the charity world. For one thing, as we have seen, charities are competing in the wrong areas. Competition in charities is all around fundraising, its channels and audiences, rather than about innovation. There is no competitive culture around providing the best possible service for beneficiaries because there is no feedback loop direct from beneficiaries and there is little shared evidence of effective interventions. As a result, there is little evidence of charities looking to acquire other charities (or to 'merge' as it is always termed in the charity sector) to build their market share. As Gugelev and Stern state:

> The nonprofit sector also lacks the kind of incentive structure that would promote scale-enhancing mergers and acquisitions. There are no shareholders to reap the benefit of such transactions. Instead, there are senior managers, who often have little to gain and much to lose when two organizations become one.
> (Gugelev and Stern 2015: 42)

Digital First or Last?

Many charities have been dragged, reluctantly, into the digital world. After years of protesting that their work could only be done on paper, or face to face, the Covid-19 crisis revealed overnight just how many areas of charity work could be done virtually, digitally, with actually relatively little cost (CAF 2020). For too many charities, though, digital is still just perceived as a channel. It is just the use of email, or text message to send out the same sort of monthly newsletter or it is just replacing leaflets in doctors' surgeries with a website. Charities have not yet, with a few exceptions, seen digital as an opportunity to creatively re-imagine the way that they run: 51% of charities still lack a digital strategy and 48% see staff skills as a major barrier to improving their digital work (Skills Platform et al. 2020: 9). When charities were asked which areas of work they prioritised for digital development the top two were fundraising (41%) and communication channels (50%) (ibid.: 10).

There is a plethora of digital opportunities available to charities, and there is real certainty that the future expectations of beneficiaries and donors will be rooted in digital experience. Even if charities cannot yet see the positive potential in digital, if they had the opportunity to reflect on their future direction, many would surely recognise that this is a radical change they need to get ahead of. Of course there are the obvious barriers around the affordability of new technology, but there is also a deeper cultural issue. Re-thinking how, and what, charities deliver, when faced with such a revolutionary change is challenging. It means re-thinking prized services and it also means recognising that having a passion for the cause is not enough: in digital development, as in other areas of charities' work today, there is a need for specialist expertise in the use of data, digital marketing, databases and software systems.

This is one stark example of where passion for the cause, or what Clara Miller refers to as 'sweat-equity', will not help charities (Miller 2003). Charities need to employ people who are trained and skilled in these specialist areas, and they need to think through the implications for their beneficiaries and themselves of this great technological shift. This takes time, but it also takes a certain culture: a willingness to look up and look outside, to learn from others and imaginatively re-invent services for tomorrow.

Running Charities for the Future

While small, local, alms-giving charities may continue to flourish in an old-fashioned culture of sacrifice and altruism, if we do want charities to be able to recognise and tackle emerging social and environmental issues, they need to be free to operate in a way that is responsive to a rapidly changing world. Charities need to be able to employ people with the skills and experience they need to deliver truly high quality services. Charities should have the working capital to trial different approaches and to robustly evidence the effectiveness of their initiatives and, crucially, they should be able to invest in the infrastructure to scale responses.

This means releasing charities from the cultural and contradictory expectations that bind them. It means supporting charities to build up their working capital to be able to invest in research and experimentation to develop the best possible interventions. It means an acceptance that efficiency is not simply a question of low costs. And these problem-solving charities need to accept that they cannot always be paragon organisations. Charities need to recognise that they will always need to make ethical trade-offs about the way in which they operate, and not to get too distracted by the latest mini-controversy which provokes headlines about the sector.

When deciding on these trade-offs in how to run a charity, leaders and trustees constantly need to ask themselves the question: is this in the best interests of our beneficiaries? Then charities need to be given the space, and the trust, to invest where they see fit, to ensure that the work they do is the most effective it can be. This is likely to mean rejecting misconceptions around professionalisation in the sector, and challenging the prevalent view that charities should somehow be able to rely on passion, hard work and goodwill instead of professional skills and investment. Charities will need to persuade their donors that managers and specialist staff and innovation are worth the investment.

Charities do not only need to persuade their external stakeholders about their value – they also need to shake off their own diffidence. For too long charities have been defensive about staff pay, the amount they invest in running excellent services and in developing the best services for tomorrow. Charities should not feel the need to shy away from these arguments: charities themselves need to better value the important contribution they make and invest in their operations appropriately.

6

SHOULD CHARITIES BE RUN BY VOLUNTEERS OR PAID STAFF?

CASE STUDY: EYEWITNESS TO ATROCITIES APP

At lunchtime in a smart law firm near the Barbican in London lawyers and support staff take time out of their busy schedules to volunteer … at their desks. The EyeWitness to Atrocities app is a portal where images and video footage of human rights violations can be securely uploaded and their authenticity verified. This material is reviewed by pro bono lawyers at the international law firm Linklaters and then sent back to EyeWitness, enabling the footage to be used as evidence in investigations and prosecutions. Eye-Witness is just one volunteer-on-demand opportunity that opens up the possibility of expert volunteering to those unable to spare time to travel to make a difference by using their valuable professional expertise. This is truly 21st century volunteering: online, on demand and available at the click of a mouse.

(Linklaters 2018)

We often refer to charities as 'the voluntary sector', a term which places volunteers at the centre of what we do. It refers back to the charity sector's rich history and to the very definition of the word charity (Dees 2012). This idea of caring, altruistic volunteers reflects a kind of archetypal charity. One that is run entirely by caring volunteers, in which a donation would go direct to the beneficiary, without the need to pay anyone to deliver this service.

DOI: 10.4324/9781003139089-6

There are still plenty of supporters of the idea that charities should be run in this way – by altruistic volunteers and without any, or many, core costs. These views can be heard in today's discussions and soul-searching about the charity sector, but they do not fit with a significant segment of the sector and its work. While 80% of charities have no paid staff, this reflects the fact that most registered charities are tiny: of the 167,000 charities in the England and Wales 81% are micro or small charities with incomes of less than £100,000, 47% actually receive less than £10,000 income per annum. The combined income of this 81% accounted for only 4% of the sector's total in 2017/18 (NCVO 2019a).

The vast majority of income in the sector is concentrated in the larger charities: charities with an income over £1m together accounted for more than 81% of the sector's total spending and 87% of its total assets in 2017/18 (NCVO 2020). The reality for these larger-income charities is that paid employees are necessary. In fact, the idea that charities were entirely run by volunteers in the past is also something of a myth: there have been paid workers in charities for longer than we might imagine. A report on political and economic planning in 1937 noted the 'growth of a salaried bureaucracy' (Smith 2019: 44) in voluntary groups, and the 1931 census recorded 10,000 people as paid workers in charities (ibid.). In 2018 the number of paid employees in charities was just over 900,000 or around 3% of the total UK workforce (NCVO 2020).

In recent years, as charities have taken on more public service contracts and greater attention has been paid to safeguarding vulnerable people, volunteers' roles have also changed. Charities now navigate funding and regulatory requirements when they decide to take on volunteers, and this has led to a shift in the types of roles where volunteers are sought.

However, while the nature of the engagement of volunteers versus paid staff has altered in some charities, public opinion has not shifted with it. Even where members of the public accept that some charity workers need to be paid and some cost is necessary to maintain the framework of a delivery organisation, this voluntarist archetype haunts non-profits. It lies behind the constant needling queries about staff salaries and, in particular, the question of whether paid staff can be replaced by volunteers. Less explicitly, the sector's history of volunteering continues to be a significant factor determining the culture and mindset of charities today, shaping also how they respond to new challenges and emerging opportunities. In this chapter I will explore what it means to have a non-profit organisation run by, or services delivered by, volunteers compared with paid staff, and what that culture of voluntarism brings to the sector today.

The Joy of Volunteering

Volunteering is assumed to be a defining characteristic of the charity sector. Ask anyone unconnected with the sector to describe a charity and I expect most would include unpaid volunteers. It is true that volunteers have a vital role to play in charities today: founders set up charities without being paid to do so, almost 20 million people volunteer each year and almost all trustees on charity boards are unpaid (NCVO 2019b: 4).

We volunteer for an enormous array of reasons and many of us feel enormously proud of, and emotionally attached to, the charity we volunteer for. The most widely cited reasons for starting volunteering are clearly emotional and values-led. People report that they volunteer 'to improve things and help people' (42%), because 'I had spare time' (38%) and because 'the organisation is really important to me' (38%) (ibid.:35). Volunteers fulfil a wide range of roles in charities with running events being the most popular, followed by administrative work and fundraising (ibid.:28).

Some of the UK's larger charities still rely on volunteers: local scouts groups are run by volunteers who are supported and trained nationally by the Scouts charity. Similarly, to cover its helplines the Samaritans relies on its group of volunteers who are trained and supported by paid staff. Certain types of roles in charities are thought to be particularly well-suited to volunteers. Examples include community outreach, where local volunteers who live in particular communities may have better reach into those communities than paid staff. This was the thinking behind the government's Health Trainers and Health Champions projects commissioned in and after 2009 (Bailey and Kerlin 2015).[1] These projects drew in volunteers from specific local communities to help disseminate messages and support to prevent poor health, on the principle that people are more likely to listen to peers than to health authorities. As Pete Alcock points out:

> It may be that there are certain 'niche' roles that are best filled by volunteers, perhaps particularly amongst groups where professionals are mistrusted, or where the fact that someone chooses to care voluntarily could have a significant impact on another's wellbeing. Volunteers may also have an important role in meeting the increasing need for culturally sensitive services that are tailored to particular ethnic or religious groups.
>
> *(Alcock 2010)*

Janet Thorne told me that she can see the difference that skills-based volunteering can make to charities with a turnover of up to £500,000 (Thorne 2020). Skills-based volunteering is significantly different from more generic volunteering. Instead of drawing in anyone, whatever their ability, to run events, paint a community centre or get sponsorship for a race, skills-based volunteering brings in new expertise to the charity. These are often skills that the charity itself couldn't afford, such as digital marketing, design or strategy, or, in the case of EyeWitness and Linklaters above, professional legal expertise.

Another obvious benefit of volunteers is in limiting a charity's cost base. Volunteers run many youth hostels, guide visitors around National Trust properties, and set up and sustain the thousands of scouts and guides groups across the country. The comparable cost of actually employing people to do these roles could make these charities unviable. Perhaps the most familiar example is the vast army of volunteers who work in charity shops across the country. These volunteers staff the shops while the charity pays a manager to recruit, train, manage rotas and so on for several different locations. This is an extremely cost-effective model which significantly limits the charity's overheads compared with other local businesses. There are currently estimated to be 11,500 charity shops across the UK (Charity Retail Association 2020), and the 600 Oxfam shops alone brought the charity a profit of £17.3m in 2018–19 (Oxfam 2019: 33).

Unsurprisingly, volunteers tend to gravitate toward volunteering which dovetails well with their existing hobbies and is fun and enjoyable, alongside fitting their skills and experience (NCVO 2019b: 8). Volunteers often bring an enthusiasm for the charity's cause, which is infectious, they may also bring with them a new network of contacts for the charity. Both of these attributes make volunteers extremely valuable to the charity fundraiser. Now that the days of cold calling and aggressive marketing are considered unacceptable across the sector, the vast majority of charities (being unable to afford the slick advertising that the super-major charities unleash) are dependent on word-of-mouth marketing. A passionate volunteer can mobilise new streams of individual giving and sponsorship in an authentic and appealing way. Just think of the volunteer force that oversees weekly Park Runs, or the 11,000 strong volunteering cadre delivering Crisis at Christmas.

There is something awe-inspiring about volunteering on this scale, and there is also something profoundly moving about regular local volunteering on the smallest scale: one of my former colleagues regularly volunteers through a local charity by simply calling round to see an older man in her neighbourhood to have a chat. Often she is the only person he speaks to for days. This is the dynamic we saw in action during the 2020 lockdown period when the Covid-19 pandemic first hit. Suddenly thousands of vulnerable people were unable to leave their homes, and some foods and goods were scarce. At the same time, many thousands of other people who were furloughed from their jobs or working from home found they had more time to give, and had more recognition of the issues on their doorstep. What followed was a mushrooming of so-called 'mutual aid'. Often through the agency of existing local organisations and businesses, people volunteered to support others in their community (Tiratelli and Kaye 2020).

Feel-Good Factor?

Beyond the money-saving and extended reach that charities are able to achieve through volunteers, there are also very real benefits to each volunteer. Numerous studies have explored the psychology of volunteering and, without citing them all, it is clear that volunteering can be a profoundly positive experience. Of volunteers, 93% say that they enjoy volunteering, with 90% saying it gives them the sense they are 'making a difference' and a sense of personal achievement (NCVO 2019b: 58).

Three-quarters of volunteers state that volunteering benefits mental health and wellbeing (ibid.: 57).

Interestingly, the benefits of volunteering to an individual's chance of gaining paid work do not feature significantly. In NCVO's survey, only 34% said they felt that volunteering improved their employment prospects. Similarly, few people report that they volunteer because they think it will help their employment prospects (ibid.: 38). This is despite significant funding being channelled into volunteering projects since 2010 with the aim of moving people who have been long-term unemployed into paid work through volunteering. This reflects research into the psychology behind volunteering, which indicates that volunteers value intrinsic above extrinsic motivation (Degli Antoni 2009). That is to say that it is the personal, values-related aspects of charity that leads individuals to volunteer, rather than extrinsic motivations (i.e. when a person stands to gain something materially through their action).

Since 2010, volunteering has been seen as a pathway to work. Post 2010, as the coalition government made significant cuts to social security provision, long-term unemployed people were pushed to get back into the labour market and volunteering was seen as a step towards this paid work. As a result, many charities were encouraged to support long-term unemployed people to volunteer with them to gain experience of employment, for example through the £1.9m Big Lottery project Volunteering for Stronger Communities from 2011–13. While this funding was welcomed as a way of supporting volunteer management roles, the transactional nature of this volunteering sat uneasily with many. This was partly because of doubts about its effectiveness, but also because it undermined the underlying culture of volunteering. It turned volunteering into something that must be done in order to receive benefits payments and this runs counter to the motivations we are familiar with in regular volunteers.

Some Societies are Bigger Than Others

Such are the benefits of volunteering to charities and to volunteers themselves that it is easy to see why the concept of volunteering is so well liked. Since the early twentieth century we have seen politicians grasp the benefits of volunteering as a mechanism to support and celebrate the active citizen and as a (cheaper) alternative to the state provision of services (Smith 2019). The most recent manifestation of this was the 2010 coalition government's Big Society initiative. This project lionised grassroots community activism (of the apolitical variety) and volunteering. It envisaged disadvantaged communities helping themselves and, conveniently for a government committed to deficit reduction, a reduced role of the state (Szreter and Ishkanian 2012).

Big Society encapsulated the fantasy of the charity: projects set up by motivated local people who were, by their very local-ness, best-placed to solve local problems. They would be volunteers, so would not require payment. They would naturally work together, inspired by a single, clear objective and without the need for any bureaucracy. They would not need to work through local authority contracts, they could develop organically, stay small and deliver meaningful change with their neighbours.

This initiative, however, failed to acknowledge some of the practical limitations of volunteering. The architects of Big Society assumed that charities pop up when and where they are needed most. However, as a subsequent audit of Big Society found, this 'social action' (volunteering and donations) does not tend to happen at the scale required and "is not reaching the parts that need it most" (Civil Exchange 2015: 5). The fact is that volunteers, like charities, are not equally available in all parts of the country, or even in all parts of the same region or city. Research by the University of Birmingham's Third Sector Research Centre (TSRC) found that "deprived areas had lower levels of both social capital and volunteering than more affluent areas" (Alcock, Butt and Macmillan 2013). This is significant because 81% of volunteers support an organisation in their local community (NCVO 2019b: 8). So, if there are not volunteers available locally charities will lack the kind of social capital that can be called up in other, more affluent, areas.

Volunteers are also far from representative. Instead, they tend to be from "…the most prosperous, middle-aged and highly educated sections of the population" (Alcock, Butt and Macmillan 2013: 30). This is backed up by NCVO research which found that people from higher socio-economic groups were more likely than those from lower ones to be both recent (44% vs. 30%) and frequent volunteers (30% vs. 19%) while those from lower socio-economic groups were most likely to say they had never volunteered (40% vs. 25%) (NCVO 2019b: 18). This is unsurprising given that those with lower incomes tend to have significantly more constraints on their time. As Alcock points out "time can be seen as a commodity or resource that is given away at a cost" so households with greater financial security are more able to 'release' one of their members for volunteering activity (Alcock, Butt and Macmillan 2013).

Volunteering has significant costs, including the opportunity cost of not having paid work instead. This was starkly illustrated in the 2011 news reports around non-payment of charity interns, which highlighted the exclusion of less wealthy young people from entry into the charity sector (de Grunwald 2011). In 2018 the Sutton Trust calculated that accepting an unpaid internship in London was likely to actually cost the intern an average of £1,019 per month (Montecute 2018). Unsurprisingly then those people who do volunteer, including interns, tend to be wealthier, whereas in general those people whom charities support tend to be less wealthy. This introduces an uncomfortable class and power dynamic to the practice of volunteering.

This imbalance of power between the volunteer and the beneficiary is not new. Victorian and Edwardian literature includes some entertaining send-ups of Lady Bountiful types. Mrs Jellyby in *Bleak House* spends all her time on "telescopic philanthropy" and being lauded by the establishment, while her own children variously fall down the stairs and get their heads stuck between railings (Dickens 1853: 82). In Gissing's *The Nether World* "two or three philanthropic ladies of great conscientiousness" take over a soup kitchen previously run by a popular working-class couple and then proceed to use the service as a means to inflict patronising moral lessons on those who turn up. They are incensed when their beneficiaries reject their watery soup and demand their money back "with proud independence of language". The philanthropic ladies lament this lack of gratitude and Gissing mocks them roundly:

> You have entered upon this work with the expectation of gratitude? …
> Have you still to learn what this nether world has been made by those who
> belong to the sphere above it?
>
> *(Gissing 1889: 252)*

This paternalistic culture, in which those in Gissing's 'sphere above' dominate, endures in some charities today. The former CEO of a grant-making trust spoke to me of her frustration at the sector's attitudes:

> [the sector] still has a 'doing to' mindset. Especially in relation to older peo-
> ples' services where [older people] are infantilised. This … fails to recognise
> that people don't want to ask for help, or don't want the type of help on
> offer. Increasingly people want agency.
>
> *(Interviewee V 2020)*

This mismatch between those volunteering and those in need brings into question volunteers' ability to be able to deliver on one of the most valuable potential aspects of volunteering – extending a charity's reach in certain communities.

Another area of inequity in volunteering relates to the type of cause that attracts volunteers. This, perhaps unsurprisingly, reveals similar trends to charitable giving: volunteers follow their own personal preference and interest and are guided by emotion rather than by any consideration of greatest need and effectiveness. As Alcock concludes:

> Much voluntary activity is oriented towards meeting needs for social inter-
> action and enjoyment, not necessarily towards meeting policy goals
> (although these may at times overlap).
>
> *(Alcock, Butt and Macmillan 2013: 30)*

Data shows that the most popular areas of involvement for formal volunteers were sports and exercise (52%); hobbies, recreation, arts and social clubs (40%) and children's education/schools (34%) (ibid.). These causes are certainly socially valuable, but are not reflective of where the needs are greatest.

Outgrowing Volunteers

In addition to limits on the availability of volunteers there are further limitations on the extent to which volunteering, and volunteer preferences, support the operational models of charities today. As we have seen, when charities grow and formalise, they move from being loose groups of informal volunteers to become organisations. Charities delivering commissioned services are less likely to take on volunteers, as research into the impact of commissioning on homelessness charities shows:

> those [charities] that were heavily dependent on contractual income did not tend to involve volunteers in core service provision roles [...]. As [the charities] take on an increasing role in the delivery of front line health and social care to vulnerable people, the professional responsibilities involved often mitigate against the use of volunteers.
>
> *(Alcock, Butt and Macmillan 2013: 31)*

It is not surprising that contracting charities are less likely to work with volunteers. The professional responsibilities required of charities taking on frontline health and social care support for vulnerable people are considerable, and require significant training as well as accountability. Some of the training and obligations this places on volunteers would make it difficult for charities to make the case that these volunteers are not workers, and not therefore entitled to payment under the National Minimum Wage Act. This definition of worker/volunteer is a grey area and one which charities have to negotiate very carefully (Volunteering England 2003).

Equally, volunteers are often unenthusiastic about being managed in a more structured way by a volunteer coordinator. In those charities which employed volunteer managers the volunteers were more likely to complain that volunteering felt 'too much like paid work' (NCVO 2019b: 48). Also, the majority of volunteers report that they like to be able to 'dip in and out' of volunteering with only 30% happy to make a regular commitment (ibid.: 72). This preference for flexibility and contributing (entirely understandably) on their own terms, points to some of the difficulties in harnessing volunteers to deliver specific, timebound pieces of work which have to be done in a very specific way and to a specific standard.

I know this from my own experience at Carers Network. Supporting unpaid carers can be extremely challenging, as well as rewarding, work and it is not well paid. Support workers may uncover complex issues within the household and, following a shift to delivering local authority commissioned contracts, the charity was responsible for completing statutory carers assessments with unpaid carers. Not only do these require significant training to complete and professional management to oversee, but considerable emotional support also needs to be provided for workers who need to debrief on their experiences. Would it be right to ask a volunteer to do this work? And would it be right to rely on a volunteer (who has no written contract with the charity and has a legal right to give up volunteering on the morning of an appointment, should they wish to) to take on this responsibility to support a vulnerable person? The Carers Network team was sure that this was not appropriate. It did not fit with the legal definition of a volunteer and the risks to both the volunteer and the service users were too great.

What is more, this area of work did not fit with volunteers' preferences and motivations. Volunteers wanted to dip in and out of the hours they volunteered, they wanted flexibility, they wanted enjoyment – not necessarily responsibility.

Leading Volunteers

As we have seen, one of the attractions of running a service through volunteers is economic. Some people imagine that this is a way of running services for free, or next to nothing. It is not unusual to come across trustees who are adamant that a charity could not only recruit a team of volunteers for no cost, but that the manager for these volunteers could also be a volunteer role. While this may work in some rare circumstances, anyone who has run a charity knows that volunteers need management, and management requires resource.

Volunteers do not have to turn up whenever you need them, and they are not naturally able to anticipate the charity's needs and slot into its culture. Volunteers need some coordination and ongoing management: although it is not possible to oblige volunteers to turn up at a specific time and place, they need to have their expectations about hours planned and their behaviour overseen so that it is in line with that of the organisation. The reality is that working with volunteers does not come without cost. It requires two things that most charities lack most of all: management time and experience.

Persuading volunteers to do the work that the organisation actually needs to get done is an art. Some volunteer coordinators are brilliant at this, some organisations manage this really well, but it cannot be taken for granted. Volunteers are, after all, supporting a charity because they want to, not because they have to. As a result they have a very different relationship with their host organisation to that of a paid member of staff. Some fascinating research has been done on this relationship, which sheds considerable light on the experience of managing volunteers and paid employees in the charity sector. Liao-Troth defines this relationship as the "psychological contract" that "captures the informal reciprocal agreement of a work environment", from the perspective of the individual. This contract:

> addresses what employees feel they owe the organisation and what they feel the organisation owes them, beyond issues that have been agreed upon in a formal employment contract. Volunteers are not formal employees, but the psychological contract conceptually is not restricted to paid employees.
>
> *(Liao-Troth 2005)*

The psychological contract is not agreed with anyone else, and so it enables a volunteer, and often also a charity employee, to project their own idea of what this relationship may be. Also, crucially, it identifies a volunteer's alignment with the goals of the organisation "which transcends the organisation to the goals the organisation is trying to achieve" (Liao-Troth 2005: 511).

In the charity world volunteers and many staff are inspired to support a particular charity not because they love the way it is run, but because they have a passion for the cause. This is the passion that drives volunteers to give up their time for free, and it is what drives employees to work for low salaries and do unpaid overtime. It is the very passion that for-profit businesses would covet, and which they are willing to spend significant amounts of money on consultants to try to replicate in their own culture. But this passion can bring with it different challenges: although volunteers (and many staff) feel a passion for a specific cause, this passion does not always manifest itself in agreement with, and acceptance of, all the decisions of a charity's management.

An individual volunteer may love a charity's mission to end loneliness, but their enthusiasm may not encompass the way in which the charity is going about that mission. When there is an equivalent lack of buy-in from paid members of staff a charity has some leverage, a line manager steps in and professional work objectives push the member of staff in the same direction as the rest of the charity. But with volunteers this leverage is less overt and it is weaker. A volunteer's psychological contract can inspire them to follow their heart rather than the instructions laid down by the charity. They can even feel that they have a stronger connection to and understanding of the charity's true mission and beneficiaries than the paid staff and management team.

This concept of the psychological contract helped me to understand the instances in my own experience, where volunteers clustered around certain activities in the charities I have worked in (coffee mornings) and gave others a wide berth (data collection). These were the activities that aligned with their sense of what they were there to do. It also explained why I might occasionally overhear volunteers over-sharing their own problems and offering all sorts of idiosyncratic words of wisdom to vulnerable service users who had rung up for advice. All were well-meaning actions from the volunteers, based on their (unspoken) understanding of what they were there to do – a direct connection with the cause – but potentially very damaging to the service user, and to the charity. Volunteers' enthusiasm can be wonderful, but it can also be unpredictable. That is the kind of risk that many charities, as they grow, cannot afford to take.

Growth and Expertise

Growing larger requires a wider range of staff expertise, including the professional and specialist skills involved in running an organisation. As we have seen, this involves a certain amount of gearing for growth, ensuring that the organisational infrastructure keeps pace with, or ideally anticipates, turnover and staffing growth. This is another area where the culture of the non-profit sector contrasts dramatically with that of the for-profit world, as Clara Miller observes:

> A colleague who heads the nonprofit side of a hybrid nonprofit/for profit computer consulting firm explained, "The difference between me and my

for-profit counterpart is that he instinctively overstaffs operations for growth, and I instinctively understaff in the same management situation".

(Miller 2005)

Not only are charities usually chronically under-staffed for growth, they are often under-skilled and, in order to grow organisations successfully, volunteers or staff with great passion may need to be exchanged, or at least counterbalanced, with staff with experience and specialist skills.

> To get off the ground, the organization has to have one person who can do a million different things. But then that person's limitations keep the organization from expanding.
>
> *(Hwang and Powell 2009)*

This need to grow and professionalise narrows both the opportunities available for volunteers, and the bandwidth amongst staff to recruit, support and manage volunteers.

To Pay or Not to Pay

Paying charity workers has brought significant benefits for the sector. For one, the move to pay staff has significantly increased the diversity of the sector. Paying staff has enabled charities to move beyond the paternalism which Gissing satirises in *The Nether World*, by widening the group of people who can afford to work in a charity. As Justin Davis Smith notes in his history of the NCVO:

> Paradoxically, it is professionalisation … which has been the subject of such intense criticism, that played a key part in the democratisation of (charities). So long as the leadership of charities was the sole preserve of unpaid volunteers, it was inevitable that individuals of private means would dominate. The growth of a salaried professional cadre opened opportunities for a broader cross-section of society to get involved and take on leadership roles.
>
> *(Smith 2019: 272)*

However, even where staff are paid, they can expect to earn significantly less in a charity than they would elsewhere. This may be contrary to public perception and tabloid headlines, but pay in the charity sector is low, and the more senior the role the greater the gap between the voluntary and the private and public sectors. This reflects an element of sacrifice or discount that charity workers are expected to take in their salary. As the Inquiry Into Charity Senior Executive Pay found:

> we saw evidence that this discount (on wages for charity leaders) already exists for the vast majority of paid charity leaders, giving them on

average between 25% and 45% less pay than they could command elsewhere.

(NCVO 2014a: 4)

The ongoing headlines and hand-wringing about the level of pay of a tiny handful of charity CEOs deflects the public's attention and discourages us from examining the real fact of wages in the sector, which are worryingly suppressed. As a result, the discourse on charity pay rarely touches on the impact that low wages have on charities' ability to deliver the best services.

It is possible to see this low-wage culture in charity job adverts, where CEOs are sought part-time only, and for paltry salaries (one of my interviewees described taking on a job turning around a charity in the north of England for just £24,000 a year for four days a week – an immense amount of stress for a salary that barely covered her mortgage). It can also be seen in the data produced by the Living Wage Foundation, which found that a higher percentage of charity workers are low paid (26.2%) than the average across all other sectors in the UK workforce (22%) (Living Wage Foundation 2017: 8). What is more, this proportion of low paid workers rose to 45.5% for charity workers in the residential care sector – an appalling insight into the squeeze on wages for those working in charities and delivering care for the most vulnerable.

The reasons behind this low pay in the charity sector are multiple and inter-related. Often they relate to contracts commissioned at below full cost recovery and low levels of grant income. But there is a wider cultural phenomenon here also, which valorises frugality, stems from the charity sector's history of voluntarism and is entrenched by the misleading 'comparison' style publications and websites, which we encountered earlier.

The Hairshirt Culture

A culture of sacrifice and voluntarism can persist in charities long after they have employed staff and significantly professionalised their operations. This culture, which I have come back to again and again this book, continues to influence both charity donors and charities themselves. It can shape the way in which charities operate, inspiring guilt in those that spend anything other than the bare minimum. This reliance instead on 'sweat equity' has a major impact on how charities employ and reward their staff, and how they structure their organisations. As Clara Miller explains:

> Managers, employees and funders share the belief that energy, willpower, stamina, and enthusiasm can overcome all obstacles, and that where it does not, some sort of personal failing is to blame. But what works for small organizations rarely works for larger, more complicated institutions, and vice versa. In other words, "sweat equity," and an organizational culture (and capacity) driven mainly by stamina or enthusiasm, does not scale well.
>
> *(Miller 2003)*

Donors and the public are nervous about charities paying competitive wages to their staff. The Charity Commission found that concern about CEO salaries was one of the major factors that donors cited when making a donation decision (Populus and Charity Commission 2018). However, it is not only funders who are responsible for this culture, the charity sector itself has internalised this hair-shirt mentality. Charities and their trustees are nervous about appearing profligate, they find it difficult to justify higher salaries and decent pension contributions for their staff because, as a sector, they have internalised the belief that people should be working because of their passion for a cause, not for a career.

The founder of the short-lived True and Fair Foundation, Gina Miller, was one of the angriest voices on this issue. In 2013 she criticised the salaries paid to some charity employees and said there were too many "careerists" in the sector. She was particularly critical of those charity employees who:

> moved between roles simply to climb the career ladder and get larger salaries, not because they were passionate about the causes.
>
> *(Pudelek 2013)*

On the face of it, this emphasis on a passion for a cause does seem commendable. It is often argued that the charity sector is different and that people come to work in it because they care. For those people who do have Miller's 'passion' for 'the cause' there is something distasteful about a fellow worker who also admits to wanting something for themselves, be that a challenge, some training, some seniority, additional experience, or a pay rise. There is also something uncomfortable perhaps about thinking that in a passion-for-the-cause industry, workers' skills might be transferable, and that each of us who work for charities might be replaceable.

Limited Horizons

It is possible to see this attitude reflected in the mystification of 'the cause' in job descriptions. A flick through any charity jobs recruitment site will reveal the emphasis on knowledge of a particular theme in the non-profit sector (older people, vulnerable children, health and social care) on a par with, or perhaps even above, any specific skills set. Even at CEO level there is almost always a requirement to demonstrate passion for, and knowledge of the cause, and this is prioritised above transferable skills.

Dan Corry has identified the narrowness of charity leadership experience as a real risk to the sector (Corry 2020b), something I recognised from my own experience. Reflecting on my own career I can see that former colleagues involved in social justice work tend to stay in those organisations, those working for older peoples' causes or mental health charities tend to stay in those or allied causes. Few charity employees cross over from homelessness charities into, say, animal welfare, international development, the arts or sport. Even within the charity sector, then, wide experience and cross-fertilisation is extremely limited. This carries with it the risk of the sector being too inward-looking, promoting from within and hiring managers within the same sub-set of charities. This also means that charities may miss out on potential talent and new insights from other types of charities, let alone from the private and public sectors.

Ambition in the sector, as Gina Miller's comments illustrate, is frowned upon. But discouraging individual ambition also risks the corollary of discouraging organisational ambition. While charities may be dismissive of the motivations of private sector companies, an element of competition and rewarding personal achievement should help to drive an ambitious culture. Many charity employees are extremely talented and have huge potential, but they do also have their own mortgages to pay and their own ambitions. There are opportunities for charities to channel these individual ambitions, but charity culture and structures do not always nurture and encourage these talents. Instead there is a tendency to assume, unrealistically, that charity employees are motivated by 'the cause' alone. As one charity sector employee stated in Sonia's Sodha's series of interviews with the sector:

> We are not a sector of purely selfless saints: human nature is much more complex than that, and people go into the sector because they want to do good but also for a huge variety of reasons, including wanting a fulfilling career, personal development, and to build their own profile and reputation for doing good. Are we honest enough about this?
>
> *(Sodha 2016: 35)*

Training and Development

Another manifestation of this 'hairshirtism' is charities' failure to invest in staff training and development. This is particularly difficult for smaller charities to do, as funders rarely cover the costs and it can be difficult to release staff from delivering services to spend time in training. In 2020 I attended an event with CEOs from across the sector to hear from the CEO of one of the UK's largest charities. She urged us to take up every opportunity that came our way for training, and went on to detail how her time at a business school doing an MBA and then at an Ivy League university had been critical to her progress into senior charity roles. A national charity had paid for her to do these training programmes, but an MBA can easily cost over £80,000 in fees. I found myself looking around the others in the room and wondering how many of them had been offered training opportunities like that in the charity sector. I am fairly confident that not one of them had.

This is echoed in research by Clore, which found a 'hard core' of 10% of organisations in the wider economy which do no leadership development, but that the comparable figure for charities in their survey was significantly larger, at

30% (57% of medium-sized respondents). So charities are three times more likely to overlook the development of their leadership team (Harries 2016).

Of course, it is possible to be a great charity manager and CEO without having an MBA, but the more general lack of investment in training and development underscores a wider problem. The sector misses out on a valuable infusion of new ideas about management, about digital strategy, about gearing for growth and about general financial management. More qualified staff also move around, spreading this knowledge across the sector: for example, the Centre for Charity Effectiveness notes that 86% of their graduates are promoted or move to a more senior role within three years of completing their degree.

The for-profit world is progressing at a rapid pace into a new technological era, but the charity sector lags behind. The lack of investment in training existing staff, and a charity's inability to pay enough to hire staff from other sectors with up-to-date skills and experience, holds charities back from growing great organisations and from running great organisations successfully. It is a false economy. The fact is that charities often are not able to afford to hire great people, or they are nervous about being seen to make expensive appointments. Charities may also baulk at hiring those with transferable skills from other sectors, because of the 'stickiness' of particular causes. As a result charities are not always able to hire the best, and, even when they do, a charity's culture may hamper those individuals' ambition and development.

A Future for Volunteering Without Voluntarism

Despite the association of volunteering with the charity sector's past, the trends around volunteering for the future look exciting. New forms of volunteering are emerging and different people are giving their time and skills for causes they care about. Tomorrow's volunteers however will want to do different things in different ways. They can, and they are, making a difference in new ways – campaigning organisations are developing new methods of volunteering that engage thousands online and offline – supporting calls for change. New ways of virtual working will open up the possibility of skills-based volunteering across geographical boundaries, which has the potential to bring new resources and expertise to those in more disadvantaged communities. Technologies for coordinating resources have the potential to enable volunteers to make the best use of their time, and to allocate resources when and where they are needed most. Volunteers will not want to be given job descriptions but will expect to be engaged in a way that works for them, directly connecting with the charity's mission rather than its Key Performance Indicators.

But taking advantage of these emerging opportunities requires that charities cast aside the old culture of voluntarism, with its expectation of sacrifice and frugality. Whilst charities, like any organisation, should aim to control costs, failing to invest in staff, their development, retention and expertise will prove to be a false economy. Freeing up charities to pay what they need to, in order to hire people with 21st century skills (whether or not they have any experience of the cause) will provide them with the insights, experience and imagination to re-develop their work for the major social and technological changes we face.

Note

1 Little information remains about these projects, less than a decade later, but this eva-luation gives a helpful overview.

7

WHO LEADS CHARITIES?

CASE STUDY: KIDS COMPANY

In August 2015 probably the best-known face of the charity sector, Camilla Batmanghelidjh, CEO of Kids Company, a multi-million pound charity, was unable to pay her staff the next month's salary. Suddenly the public became aware that this high-profile charity was about to go into liquidation. The newspapers showed shocked and tearful staff clearing their desks and talking about the devastating impact on the children they supported.

Gradually though a bigger story emerged: the charity had received £3m of emergency funding direct from central government to pay its previous payroll. Not only that, in the previous two years it had received almost £17m of 'direct and uncompetitive' grants from central government. Astonishingly, it had been able to circumvent all formal funding routes due to its "unique, privileged and significant access to senior Ministers and Prime Ministers" (House of Commons 2016). Despite this, the charity had failed to build up its cash reserves from just over £400,000 to the £12 million level its auditors recommended to cover six months' operating costs.

What is more, although Kids Company claimed to be supporting 36,000 people in its 2011 annual report, when files from its services were finally handed over to local authorities it emerged that the total number of young people it had been supporting was just 1,909. Inexplicably, those who agreed to fund it, including central government, did not seem to have required the charity to produce robust data on its impact, data which other charities are routinely required to provide for grants at a tiny fraction of these values.

DOI: 10.4324/9781003139089-7

The charity was unravelling quickly and, presiding over all of this was a group of extremely qualified and able trustees: the Chair was the Creative Director of the BBC and others included senior leaders from the private sector and a senior lawyer. With such high-quality trustees in such a high-profile charity, people wondered, how could this have happened? What the House of Commons report uncovered was a disaster of leadership. Somehow, the complexities of charity leadership had allowed the Founder-Chief Executive to exercise complete control over the organisation. In the view of the House of Commons Committee the trustees were held chiefly responsible.[1] They were found to have "suspend(ed) their critical faculties" and failed to protect the interests of the charity. Their lack of experience in the areas of Kids Company's work left them "unable to interrogate the decisions" of Batmanghelidhj. Furthermore, the report explicitly criticised the length of the Chief Executive's tenure (19 years) and that of the Chair (9 years) which "were not conducive to challenging the Chief Executive herself" (House of Commons 2016).

The example of Camilla Batmanghelidhj gives the impression that charity chief executives have immense power over the work and development of charity. In fact the CEO is just one of several actors sharing the leadership of a charity, and a well-functioning charity requires all these voices to be heard and balanced. While the responsibility stops with the CEO, full authority for decision-making often does not. The amount of power which a CEO holds within a charity varies enormously, it is not a given. A CEO's authority and boundaries are carefully negotiated, these differ from charity to charity and may fluctuate at different times in the charity's lifecycle.

This uncertainty around power and decision-making matters, because charities today need to be able to respond quickly to changing circumstances. Charities need to be able to change course rapidly, and a leader's ability to make decisions and see them through is vital to running, and being able to change the direction of, an organisation. The role of a charity CEO is complex. Some academics have suggested that it is more complex than comparable roles in business, because charity CEOs need not only to manage more complex tasks within the organisation, but also have to deal with the expectations arising from the broader context. They need "a broader skill set, character, and qualities" including being capable of "working with wide ranges of stakeholders" (Osula and Ng 2014).

This is an interesting aspect of leading a charity which is little understood from the outside. The CEO's role is to understand and manage the range of stakeholders around them and to negotiate a path with them all which is as close to the charity's mission as possible. These stakeholders include trustees, staff, volunteers, funders and service users. The range of voices involved in the leadership of a charity has the potential to ensure that a charity remains relevant, to provide helpful context and direction setting, to ensure that its work continues to serve its mission and to engage with the external world. Most of these stakeholders want to be helpful. But, as we will see, the reality of this chorus of opinion can mean that the path for decision-making is not clear. This can lead to diffusion of control and accountability, and in addition, multiple stakeholders bring not just diverse, but also competing expectations to the organisation (Osula and Ng 2014).

Charity sector leaders, then, face a unique set of challenges both because they have less scope to make and implement decisions, and because so much of their time and energy is spent managing this wide range of highly engaged stakeholders. In different charities with different histories, structures and characteristics, the extent of the CEO's decision-making power varies. The chorus of stakeholders may be more or less powerful, making the CEO's scope of authority larger or smaller. The need to manage and corral the stakeholders of a charity can seriously affect its risk taking and decision-making, which in turn makes it even more challenging for the charity to adapt and respond to a rapidly changing external environment.

The Trustees' Role

The first and most important voice amongst these stakeholders is the board of trustees. The trustees have a defined leadership role in registered charities, they are responsible in law for setting the charity's strategic direction and ensuring that the charity keeps on track, fulfilling its charitable purpose. In theory, trustees should provide the strategic authority in the organisation and delegate the day-to-day operations to the executive team (led by the CEO). In practice these lines of responsibility in many charities are blurred, with trustees taking a more operational interest in the charity's work.

This blurring of the trustees' role often varies with the size of the charity. Naturally, those charities with no paid employees will often rely on trustees to fulfil operational roles as well as their strategic governance remit. But the drift towards operational matters also depends to a large extent on the experience and expertise of the trustees, and their motivations for taking on the role. Charity trustees are almost always volunteers. They are very rarely paid, except for the reimbursement of expenses, in contrast to the remunerated non-executive directors who sit on company and public sector boards. While it is possible to pay trustees for their role in the charity (and some have argued that this would help increase the diversity of trustees, by including those who cannot afford to volunteer their time (Unwin 2019)) this rarely happens and requires specific consent from the Charity Commission.

All trustees have specific duties that are set out by the Charity Commission. They are responsible for ensuring that the charity is providing its public benefit and complying with its own governing documents. Trustees are required to manage the charity's resources responsibly and to always act in the charity's best interests (Charity Commission 2018). Each charity is run according to its own rules set out in its governing document, which have to be approved by the Commission. In addition, the Commission also publishes lots of (quite accessible) guidance for trustees about how to run a charity.

However, as trustees take on these roles in a part-time and voluntary capacity, the extent to which they study their responsibilities, and indeed the amount of time they actually spend thinking about the charity, vary enormously. For many trustees, reading the papers directly before a board meeting, and attending meetings for a few hours four times a year is all they are able, or required, to do. A review of charity trustees by the Centre for Charity Effectiveness estimated that the average trustee spent less than five hours a week on their trustee duties (Charity Commission et al. 2017). Although trustees themselves report being well informed about their legal duties, the Charity Commission's own report cast some doubt on this:

> Our findings suggest that there might be something of a gap between a trustee's perception of and actual knowledge of their legal duties.
>
> *(ibid)*

This amounts to a worrying sign that trustees are overstating the extent of their understanding and that many simply do not realise how much they do not know.

Trustee Recruitment

The effectiveness of trustees varies enormously. While trustees are supposed to set the strategy for the organisation, most of the CEOs I spoke to, in particular those running small to mid-sized charities, felt that this was not the case. There was a perception amongst some of the CEOs that trustees can be a hindrance rather than a help, a group whom the paid staff have to humour. Those CEOs who told me they had great trustee boards emphasised how fortunate they were, or how much work had gone into developing these boards, implying that a high-performing board was the exception rather than the rule in the sector.

As most CEOs of small to mid-sized charities will tell you, good trustees – with relevant experience and interpersonal skills – are like the proverbial gold dust. Charities struggle to recruit trustees with the right range of skills and abilities to fill their boards: Getting On Board, a charity which specialises in getting people to apply to be trustees for the first time, estimates that at any one time over half of UK charities are carrying trustee vacancies (Getting On Board 2017). This means that charities are under such pressure to recruit or retain trustees that they may end up with some trustees who are not well-suited to the role. They may also simply be unable to recruit trustees with important skills, such as an understanding of charity finance or fundraising.

A limited pool of people apply to be trustees and the profile of trustees remains predominantly older, white, male, more highly educated and middle class. Men outnumber women two to one among trustees generally, and also in the senior roles of chair and treasurer (Charity Commission et al. 2017). In addition, many of the same trustees are recycled across multiple charities, with a quarter of all trustees holding more than one trustee position (ibid). This concentration of trustees within certain demographics may be explained to some extent by the types of role that trustees are asked to play – effectively a senior management role – and the types of people who might feel confident putting themselves forward for this type of responsibility. This concentration is also likely to result, at least in part, from the way in which trustees are recruited:

> Characteristically [charities] are found to be overly reliant upon fellow trustees for both recruitment of new trustees and for their principal sources of advice and support.
>
> *(Charity Commission et al. 2017)*

With 90% of trustee positions simply never advertised (Getting On Board 2017), Penny Wilson believes that there is a much wider potential pool of trustees, but most people simply do not think about applying for trustee roles until asked, and they are less confident about having the required skills. Wilson explains that some charities are reluctant to put time and effort into trustee recruitment, and that existing trustees can harbour a fear that open recruitment might mean being overwhelmed by 'the great unwashed' (Wilson 2020).

This limited pool of trustees reduces the diversity of backgrounds, skills and experience on a charity board, increasing the risk that its views may become myopic, limiting healthy challenge and affecting decision-making (Charity Commission et al. 2017). I have heard about many examples of this limited expertise and perspective through my conversations with other charity leaders. One particularly depressing example was a CEO of a mid-sized charity whose trustees were all loosely connected friends and many were members of the same local club. The trustees loved being associated with the charity, but were not prepared to spend time doing the tough work behind the scenes. When Covid-19 struck, the board refused to meet more regularly to make the quick decisions needed, and when the CEO embarked on an attempt to refresh the board with new members they dug their heels in. After the charity's first open recruitment for new trustees, the existing trustees ran the interview process and insisted on taking on two further acquaintances from their club above other candidates.

It is perhaps instinctive for trustees to be reluctant to alter the status quo, but it is also crucial to the development and success of a charity that there is regular turnover of trustees to aid diversification. This was the reasoning behind the inclusion of maximum trustee terms in the Charity Commission's Code of Governance.

Trustee Skills

Many CEOs have spoken to me about the difficulty of managing unskilled trustees who feel out of their depth and who take refuge in detail, focusing on small line items because the bigger numbers and wicked problems are too over-whelming to grasp. For example, a board of trustees may prefer to review the detailed drafting of policies at board meetings, rather than engage in challenging discussions about a charity's strategic direction or finances.

For inexperienced, part-time trustees, strategic decision-making focused around the areas of the greatest risk can seem less interesting to trustees (because it takes them away from the service delivery aspects of the charity which may have inspired them to get involved with the charity) and it can only cause them to feel out of their depth. This is understandable. As trustees may spend very little time within the organisation, they may have little awareness of its complexity, they may have little or no training about being a trustee and this may be their first experience of management. A trustee may well feel nervous about making big decisions about an organisation where they only have an oversight role and are not in touch with the details. In such circumstances it is easy to see why trustees might feel a strong sense of responsibility towards preserving the status quo, and could lack the experience or contextual understanding to encourage the organisation to take calculated risks, or to challenge its thinking. As Sir Harvey McGrath, a highly experienced trustee and board chair, told me:

> Trustees suffer from inertia, a lack of focus and failure to think through future options. They often lack skills, they are not strategic and end up fire-fighting.
>
> *(McGrath 2020)*

Trustees – Too Weak Or Too Strong?

Trustees can hold a charity back by exercising significant control with limited understanding, but trustee boards can also be too weak, an issue recognised by some charity leaders. One CEO told me she felt she had too much power concentrated in her role and this made her uncomfortable: "a CEO with a strong personality can easily present a partial view to the board" (Interviewee T 2020). Another agreed: 'I have a lot of autonomy and power, perhaps too much?' (Interviewee U 2020). These CEOs felt that their board did not challenge them enough because they either did not know enough about the organisation, or that trustees did not pay enough attention to their role.

This lack of challenge can occur in boards made up of senior and experienced people, just as it can with inexperienced trustees. One of the (many) issues that the public found so baffling about Kids Company was that the board of trustees was made up of so many very senior people from business and public life (House of Commons 2016). In fact the phenomenon of the senior business manager turning their business-brains off when they sit on a charity board is widely recognised across the charity sector:

Highly successful business people often leave behind their business discipline, savvy, and demands for results when they sit on nonprofit boards. They seem to think these traits are not appropriate in this setting.

(Bowen 1994, cited in Dees 2012)

This phenomenon of switching off is particularly frustrating for CEOs (and trustees) who have specifically hired people with business experience to help shift the charity's culture and systems. It can lead CEOs to resent the power that trustees have in a charity when they feel that trustees do not appear to have as much commitment to the charity as they and the staff do. One CEO, a charity founder, described some trustees as "people dabbling in the sector which they know little about" and being "disrespectful of our expertise and knowledge. They wouldn't do this in any other sector!" (Interviewee W 2020).

The reality is that trustee boards often rely on the CEO to set direction. Where this relationship works well the CEO listens to the board's input and benefits from their challenges; excellent trustees focus on asking the right questions at the right time, and sign off the plans when they are satisfied on direction and risk rather than on detail.

User-Led Charity

As we have seen, trustees are not representative of the wider UK population, although they may be more representative of those undertaking roles of similar levels of responsibility in other sectors, such as company directors or other professionally skilled roles (Charity Commission et al. 2017: 17 and 18). But they are even less representative of the users of charities' services. There are examples of smaller charities which are run by the people who benefit from their services such Happy Baby Community, set up in 2015 and led by refugee women. This leadership can bring great strengths, as service users may have deep understanding of other beneficiaries and can help shape an organisation or service that reaches the right people in the best way. SignHealth is an interesting example of a charity that has continued to involve its service users while operating at increased scale. The £4.5m-turnover deaf-led charity employs many deaf people and engages many deaf people in its board, including through an innovative shadow board programme.

While smaller, community-based charities are more likely to draw some trustees from those who use their services, as a charity grows and professionalises it is more and more difficult to make this work. Larger charities need their trustees to have the experience and skills to oversee their increasingly complex work. These skills are not always to be found amongst those in a charity's immediate community. It may also be helpful for charities to recruit trustees with some distance from the organisation, to give a more objective view on its work.

An interesting practical example of a shift in scale requiring a shift in governance strategy is the Youth Hostelling Association.

CASE STUDY: THE YOUTH HOSTELLING ASSOCIATION

Grassroots trustees can look like a very good thing from the outside. The YHA for many years preserved a local and regional board set-up, where local representatives were voted onto a regional and then a national board, taking responsibility for setting the strategic direction of the organisation. While this was effective in ensuring that locally valued hostels continued to run, and that the executive leadership was accountable to members, this 'democracy' was partial. Only those with sufficient time would participate in the boards, and the result was that the trustees, though they had a passion for the work of the YHA, were unable to take the financial and strategic decisions necessary to move it forward.

The YHA has always been a social enterprise and from its inception it has successfully combined payment for accommodation with a voluntarist culture, where visitors helped with maintenance and volunteers managed the hostels. In order to survive it had to compete with a rapidly evolving tourist accommodation industry, with demand-led, flexible pricing, online bookings and less demand for shared rooms. This has required a significant understanding of corporate finance and the for-profit hospitality industry. Following a gradual but deep governance review and restructure over many years, its trustees today include lawyers, property managers and accountants alongside leaders from the charity sector and experts in diversity. These high calibre trustees make regular and quick decisions about investments and debt financing, which would have been impossible for the YHA's original volunteer-representative board, while still providing a strong commitment to the principles and values on which the charity was founded. A large, multi-million pound organisation needs much more than well-meaning volunteers on its board. It needs serious skills and serious commitment.

(Blake 2020)

This transformation of the YHA took many years to affect and CEO James Blake recognises a debt of gratitude to his predecessors, who spent decades bringing about this change. It was difficult to achieve because such a change, to a more professional-skills focused board, is not always popular among service users and existing trustees who must relinquish some power. Charities which have made this move may look to other ways to engage their members or service users to ensure that their voice is heard in the development of their work.

Many charities are aware of the changing power dynamics and drivers in wider society, which mean that is no longer considered acceptable for a small group of trustees from very different backgrounds (white, educated, older and middle class) to decide for beneficiaries on the services they will receive. Involving users of a service in the design and improvement of a charity's activities makes practical sense, and also responds to the ethical imperative to ensure that charities are not paternalistic. However, this involvement does not need to be done through trusteeship.

The role of the board of trustees is not intended by the Charity Commission to be democratically representative. Indeed it is also important to bear in mind that any 'representative' service users elected to a board will not necessarily be reflective of the broader group of service users, but may simply present their own personal views or those of a narrow cohort. In practice, an over-representation of service users on the board may also cause the charity to be more focused on maintaining its existing services for its existing beneficiaries, at the expense of its mission and future beneficiaries, which is contrary to their role as set out by the Charity Commission.

Trustees are required to fulfil a strategic governance role and should be recruited on the basis of their skills to do this. In many cases the expertise required for this role may happily overlap with the skills of a charity's service users. However, by thinking of the trustee board as the only opportunity for engaging service users in shaping a charity's work, there is the risk of missing other, potentially more effective routes to ensure that the people using the service have agency in how the charity develops.

There is no doubt that current and future service users have an important role to play in a charity, but this role will be different in different charities and it may not require involvement in governance of the charity. Above all charities need to be clear about why and how they want service users to be involved, a lack of clarity can undermine their role:

> 'Involvement for involvement's sake' can lead to process being prioritised over outcomes, of the activity becoming the end rather than the means. At worst, this results in tokenistic practice that damages trust and wastes people's time, mainly due to a mismatch in expectations about what the process was for.
>
> *(McLeod and Clay 2018: 6)*

Being a 'token' trustee can feel disempowering for service users who may be relegated to a patronising realm of giving 'the user point of view' on issues that the board is considering. Similar frustrations can extend to other groups appointed to the board in a purely representative way, for example trustees recruited to increase diversity of gender, age or ethnicity. To engage more diverse voices in shaping the charity's work there are other, much more effective, structures than board membership, such as board advisory panels, short-term consultation groups and co-production groups for new services.

Too often the laudable commitment to listen to service users' voices tend to drop away when circumstances are at their most challenging, and when this perspective is needed most. In a 2020 survey, when prompted 91% of charities surveyed said they thought user involvement in the design or deliveries of services was important for achieving their mission and 78% said they had changed their work as a result of user feedback. However, when asked *unprompted* to list their priorities as an organisation, engaging users was rarely mentioned by any of the charities:

> When we asked charities in an open question to name their greatest strength for achieving their mission, only 14 out of 300 charities mentioned their service users. This ranked 11th out of all the answers given, and was lower than volunteers, governance, and collaboration.
>
> *(NPC 2020)*

This suggests that many charities see user involvement in tokenistic terms – or at the very least they do not value their service users' insights as a key asset.

The Team

For the charities we focus on in this book, those with paid staff, the support of a charity staff team cannot be taken for granted. The emotional and personal commitment of charity workers means that they are often a crucial stakeholder in decision-making. For CEOs this presents:

> the unique challenge of leading a diverse workforce of paid staff and volunteers – sometimes with highly personal motivations for engaging with the work – [this suggests] a need for visionary and inspirational communication skills.
>
> *(Clore 20146a)*

Although paid staff are employed on what seems to be, on the surface, the same terms as employees in the private sector, charity workers' psychological contract with the charity means that they require a very different kind of management and involvement in decision-making. As academic Geoff Nichols points out:

> The strength of a psychological contract as exhibited by stakeholders of charities is based upon years of support and financial contributions, thus stakeholders feel they have obtained the right to be consulted in strategic matters.
>
> *(Nichols 2013)*

Employed staff may be aware, consciously or sub-consciously, of the element of sacrifice they have made for this role, and have logged what they are giving to the cause (working unpaid overtime, for a 'discounted' salary, poor pension contributions and maternity benefits and less attractive employment conditions than they could secure elsewhere). The member of staff may expect in return that the charity will, for instance, continue to run the services that they (the staff member) really value, and that staff members will have a role in the charity's decision-making.

Charity CEOs need to harness and channel the enthusiasm of these individual members of staff. They need to engage them in delivering a strategic plan, but to do so with the verve and energy that will harness, rather than kill, their passion for the cause. Tunde Banjoko did this very effectively at the London charity he founded, Making the Leap, when the charity faced significant funding cuts. By drawing the staff team together and being open about the challenges they faced, he managed to make this experience of crisis-driven change an experience that enhanced team cohesion, with staff agreeing to take cuts to their hours temporarily until new funding was secured (Banjoko 2020). This is an example of exactly the sort of inspirational communication that ACEVO sets out above.

However, this need for staff engagement can be more challenging in larger organisations and in situations where staff do not perceive a need for change. Michelle Hill experienced this when she embarked on a huge change programme, creating the new charity Talk Listen Change out of a former Relate service in Manchester. At first, the financial crisis the organisation faced, plus a significant effort put into communicating with and listening to staff, helped her to bring staff together. She consulted the staff on the changes she proposed and secured an astonishing 100% approval. However, challenges came later as longstanding-staff began to resent the changes to the charity's focus and priorities and she sensed a split in the teams between these and newer team members, which could impact morale (Hill 2020). This underlines the constant need to engage staff teams and bring them along with decision-making in charities, where staff have such high levels of identification with the cause and correspondingly high expectations about their agency in the charity's decision-making.

The Chosen Leader

The extent to which a CEO can corral and make sense of the input from this chorus of stakeholders will depend on their skills, experience and the amount of time available. Leadership skills amongst charity CEOs is a much-discussed topic in both the UK and US and the shortcomings of charity leaders have been identified as one of the aspects holding back charities:

> The lack of investment in leadership skills means that there is a small pool of appropriately skilled leaders, a continued drain of talent to the public and private sector, and a restricted pipeline of future leadership across the sector.
> *(Hodges and Howieson 2017)*

Despite this hand-wringing, which has endured now for more than a decade, commentators have noted a distinct lack of progress (Clore 2016a). Charities do not invest in leadership training, nor do they pay well enough to lure expertise in from other sectors because the sector's hairshirt mentality once again curbs the thinking of charity trustees and CEOs themselves feel guilty about investing in leadership skills (Clore 2016b).

In her review of charity leadership Mary Marsh described "the root causes" of poor leadership as lying within culture in the charity sector. One of the causes she identified was that the charity sector itself is hostile to leadership development, seeing it as "wrong and selfish". This is a view that falsely associates this investment solely with the benefit it confers to the member of staff. It fails to recognise that a more able member of staff brings huge advantages to the charity and its work, so that "all of us are collectively better off, including our beneficiaries, if we avoid this narrow thinking".

Mary Marsh also identifies a tendency within the sector to focus on existing leaders, not aspiring leaders, so that individuals with potential are not developed, and there are "too many sticks in the mud", i.e. charity leaders who stay in role for far too long, limiting the opportunities for others to progress and for new blood to bring in new thinking (Clore 2016b: 6). Marsh states that "social action leaders tend to have longer careers with one organisation" and, however talented and exceptional some of these leaders may be, it may not be healthy for the sector to cultivate such long-term leaders. While depth of experience is valuable, it is possible that long-term tenures mean that charities miss out on new ideas and a fresh perspective that might challenge them to consider doing things differently. Sometimes a new stage in a charity's development requires different skills.

This failure to invest in charity leadership has an enormous impact on the sector. It limits the tools that charity leaders have at their disposal to manage complex stake-holder relationships systematically. It also limits their ability to innovate:

> Leadership can have a strong influence on innovation in the sector and can influence new ideas and concepts for service delivery which are critical to the improvement of organizational performance in the sector. The ability to 'innovate' is, therefore, one of the key capabilities which the third sector leadership needs to develop.
>
> *(Hodges and Howieson 2017: 75)*

The sector does not just fail to invest in the leaders it already has, there are also shortcomings in its recruitment of new leaders. Many of those I spoke to for this book have privately expressed to me their dismay and frustration at the lack of leaders in the big charities who are genuinely doing things differently, who are challenging the status quo and actively preparing their charities for the future. There is a common perception that CEOs are too often promoted from within an organisation. While this ensures that the CEO has a strong understanding of the charity's activities, it limits their experience of other organisations and sectors, and misses an opportunity to challenge assumptions and identify new opportunities through a new perspective.

Sector recruiters Gatenby Sanderson undertook an interesting examination of the skills they found were needed in the coming generation of charity leaders, in which they noted a reason for the poor-quality appointments to CEO roles in the sector, which others have also mentioned to me:

When presented with candidates who think, behave, and act differently to their predecessors it is not difficult to understand why many boards choose to stick with the 'safe' option. In fact there may be greater risk in continuing to hire like for like in a sector that is so rapidly changing.

(Gatenby Sanderson undated: 14)

This risk-averse mentality reflects the challenge that is faced by boards and trustees who may not be aware of, or agreed on, the skills and experience they need to prioritise in any new CEO. CEO roles are complex, as we have seen, and it is easy to see how this lack of understanding or lack of confidence amongst a board of trustees could lead to a tendency to promote from within or to recruit like for like, resulting in a missed opportunity for a sector whose defining characteristic needs to be adaptability and innovation.

Dan Corry of NPC set out to me the benefits he believes to be derived from hiring across sector divides. In his experience of working with very many charity leaders, and through his own personal experience of working across the private, public and now non-profit sector, Corry is aware of the valuable insights gained from other sectors, and vice versa. He expressed his surprise on discovering how seldom this crossover between sector leaders happens, a point that other charity leaders echoed (Corry 2020b). One interesting aspect of this is the lack of movement between the charity and the business world. Simply taking this from a personal perspective, after 15 years of working in charities, with the exception of corporate social responsibility roles, I know of not one single individual who has made the move from an established charity role into an equivalent business role (excluding those who have set up their own businesses). I suspect such moves are highly unusual and, although beyond the scope of this book, the reasons would be interesting to explore. I suspect that charity leaders' stock just is not very high with other sectors. Charity leaders' lack of training and development may set us back in comparison with executives in the business sector, and there is also a question of the extent to which the complexity of charity roles is understood and recognised in other sectors.

These questions around how chief executives are selected and how they are, or are not, developed are fundamental to charities' ability to adapt. The CEO's role is absolutely critical to managing, and getting the most out of, the different and competing voices within a charity, all of which want to have their say about the charity's direction. Without the skills in place to lead their stakeholders, and confronted with a complex structure which takes significant expertise to navigate, a chief executive who wants to move a charity into a new phase to adapt and survive, faces an almost insurmountable struggle.

Leading the Way to 2030

The many stakeholders who vie for the leadership of charities can provide helpful checks and balances. Service users can ensure that a charity is accountable to the people it supports and provide the vital feedback loop, which charities' financial model does not provide. Members of staff can remind a charity's leadership to bring them along with any changes, a process which is much harder to do in retrospect. Trustees have the potential to play a vital, objective and strategic role, providing healthy challenge and support to the chief executive.

But too often these voices are more cacophony than choir. What is more, it is a rare and talented chief executive who has the skills to bring all of these potentially conflicting stakeholders with them, at the same time as setting a bold future direction for the organisation. Operating in such a complex environment and with a requirement to coalesce all these stakeholders around major decisions, it is unsurprising that we see charity leaders focusing less on bold and ambitious plans for the future, and more on preserving as much as possible of the status quo, where consensus is already in place and no boat-rocking is necessary.

So what would be a better way to lead non-profits? I am convinced we need to value charity leaders more highly for a start. Charities tend to have few material assets and staff are their most valuable one. Charities need to push themselves and their funders past this old-fashioned idolising of 'hairshirtism' and 'sweat equity'. If charities do want to run high-quality and sustainable organisations, they need to be able to invest in the people who will achieve this. Innovative leaders will see the problems and opportunities early and will have the skills to adapt and survive. Trustees need to think harder and be bolder about their hiring decisions, and chief executives need to value their own development and their team's training as an investment in the future of the services they are running.

I have some sympathy with the argument for paying trustees. It seems anathema to the expectations of large charities today that their governing trustees are unpaid volunteers. This may limit the people who are willing and able to give up their time to be trustees, it places non-executive director (NED) positions in the public and private sector ahead of non-profits for those seeking 'portfolio careers'. In addition, I believe that unremunerated positions may have an important psychological impact, as it may make chief executives feel less able to demand support and attention from trustees when it is needed. As with all pro bono gestures, there can be a sense that charities are scrabbling after scraps and ought to be grateful for what they are given, rather than being able to demand focus, attention and excellence from a governing board.

This pro bono mindset is no way to run a complex organisation, which at times may need to call on a lot of trustees' time in order to execute a pivot in services or structure. Paying trustees could help charities to feel that they can be more demanding of their boards. It may also concentrate trustees' minds on their role and strengthen their commitment to the charity's success. After all, as Dees points out:

> no one would suggest that Goldman Sachs, Infosys, or Unilever be led by volunteers, or by retirees from another sector looking for a "second act." Too much is at stake. Yet these ideas are commonplace ideas in the social

sector, and they trivialize the challenges of serious social problem solving. It is as if working in this sector is simply an act of kindness and generosity, not a serious challenge requiring deep expertise. When the goal is innovative, cost-effective problem solving with large- scale impact, serious talent, and deep expertise are needed.

(Dees 2012)

This proposal to pay trustees cannot, however, be divorced from the reality that many charities simply don't have the money to pay trustees (nor, frankly, would they welcome the painful bureaucratic process of getting permission from the Charity Commission to be able to do this). Funders would need to accept and support this move for larger charities, perhaps providing additional funding to make this possible.

The current diffuse nature of charity leadership tends to act as a brake on change and development. For as long as all these different stakeholders need to be brought into agreement, despite their differing levels of knowledge and commitment, charity leaders will find too much of their time taken up by trying to reconcile and inform and bring along these stakeholders, at the expense of timely decision-making.

Note

1 To note that in February 2021 the subsequent High Court ruling on the case brought by the Official Receiver to disqualify the directors took a different view, namely that it was unreasonable to place such high expectations on charity trustees and the CEO, largely because of the risk it would have of deterring highly qualified people for taking on charity trustee roles (Kids Company and the Company Directors Disqualification Act (2021).

8

HOW ARE SOME ORGANISATIONS CHANGING THE WORLD?

In this book we have explored some of the factors holding charities back from re-imagining what they could do to meet the changing needs and expectations of the world around them. But if charities were liberated from some of the factors we have identified and did want to effect change, where should they look for inspiration?

One of the fascinating aspects of this current period of rapid change is that new ways of doing things are bubbling up all around us. We do not know exactly what the future holds, of course, but it is widely accepted that climate change, an ageing population, un- or under-employment, and the increasing digitisation of our societies will be major challenges we will need to tackle. These challenges will also bring with them the requirement for charities to achieve their public benefit goals in different ways. The immediate crisis of managing the Covid-19 pandemic dominates our thinking as I write in 2021, but there are also medium- to long-term changes which this pandemic will bring about in the way we live and work.

In such a rapidly changing environment, tweaking existing services may not be enough for charities to survive, let alone to continue to be effective. As innovator and social entrepreneur Hillary Cottam puts it:

> While we focus narrowly on how to patch and mend our post-war welfare institutions our attention is diverted from the bigger social shifts and transitions that are taking place. The world that surrounds our welfare systems is very different. When we ask our questions and start our innovations from within – standing inside the institutions and wondering how they can be fixed – we miss the mismatch between what is on offer and what help is required. And crucially, we also overlook the potential that surrounds us: the new ideas, resources, inventions and energy that we could bring to the problems at hand.
>
> *(Cottam 2018)*

DOI: 10.4324/9781003139089-8

Cottam is writing about public services, but the same principles apply to the voluntary sector. There is a growing mismatch between what charities offer and the help that will be required. Those organisations which are successfully adapting to the changing world are looking around them and engaging with this change, drawing on new assets and seizing the opportunities that change can offer. They are taking a wider perspective and challenging some of their most basic assumptions.

In this chapter I will share some of the thinking and approaches being used by these organisations. They are not necessarily registered charities or even non-profits, some may even be doing work that is anathema to charity values, but this is not an endorsement of every element of their work. Instead it is intended to provoke thought and discussion, to help explore how the charity sector might go about doing things differently in order to develop more effective and relevant services and campaigns in future.

Back to Basics

We heard earlier about the process Scope went through in divesting itself of its longstanding statutory contracts, because its board felt that the charity was not able to deliver these in line with the values of the organisation and to the benefit of its service users. Barnardo's, one of the UK's larger charities, has also radically re-examined its purpose. The charity, established in 1867 with the founding principle that 'every child deserved the best possible start in life, whatever their background', has recognised that, in the 2020s, the changing world around it requires a dramatically different approach. CEO Javed Khan set out some of the thinking behind Barnardo's review process in a description that has echoes of Cottam's observations above:

> At Barnardo's we're really clear that we need a radical new approach. The children's services eco-system has to move away from short-term thinking, siloed decision-making and the traditional transactional relationships that are underpinned by a competitive scramble, towards long-term, sustained interventions that can actually transform the life chances of the most vulnerable children in our society.
>
> To drive this new way of thinking and acting, we're developing strategic partnerships. We are helping to bring together partners including national government, local authorities, the police, the NHS and, crucially, families and communities to co-design, co-create and co-deliver the services children really need, with a strong emphasis on prevention.
>
> *(Khan 2018)*

Barnardo's aims to establish its own foundation, to give grants to the projects that make the biggest difference. Not only will it ask its own internal teams to compete for this funding, it will also fund partners' projects and joint projects from this pool of unrestricted cash (Barnardo's 2019: 7). This is significant not only because of Barnardo's plans to fund other organisations' work as well as their own, but because it creates a different dynamic internally. This foundation looks set to introduce an element of competition for funds within the organisation but, crucially, this competition will be based on impact. Projects will need to demonstrate their effectiveness in order to succeed. This embeds a very different level of focus on impact and accountability through the charity's culture.

For a traditional charity like Barnardo's this is a fundamental shift in culture. Barnardo's is attempting to introduce a greater degree of transparency and accountability to its work, as well as attempting to reach outside its own organisation to support other initiatives. Nowhere is this more apparent than in the charity's fascinating blog. Here it shares experiences of developing new services and other internal services. Director of Design, Digital and Transformation, Jason Caplin, admits that Barnardo's will not have all the answers itself, but the charity believes that others are also asking the same questions and "We think it'll be better to answer the hard questions together". He describes his collaboration with Barnardo's staff, service users, external professionals and supporters as "the collective brain we can tap into for advice" and emphasises the different relationship they are trying to embed: "We're listening. We want this blog — and by extension, all our work — to be a conversation, not a press release" (Caplin 2019).

Interestingly, at the time of writing Caplin describes himself as a "cheerleader" on his twitter account. For those unfamiliar with the concept of New Power, this is a term to describe a new generation of leaders who work within existing organisations but adopt so-called new power values, like transparency and collaboration. The idea of this kind of radical openness and collaboration, operating as a kind of umbrella or platform for organisations trying to achieve the same goals, is a compelling concept. Earlier we saw Crisis trying to achieve a similar affect through its increasing collaboration with other, local homelessness organisations across the UK. Jon Sparkes described the charity as looking to take inspiration from outside and to invest in better understanding which models work well. Crisis wants to invest in those interventions which have the greatest impact and then share these with the wider world, to inspire government and other charities to emulate:

> We take inspiration from outside and [it's important to] give up control and share what works. …. We also want to share concepts so that others can learn from our work [and we can learn from theirs], set up and run projects that work.
>
> *(Sparkes 2020)*

This kind of collaboration and partnership though requires some ceding of control.

'It's Only a Movement if it Moves Without You'

Giving away power over the results and outcomes of a piece of work is a common concept in contemporary entrepreneurship. As Marina Gorbis of the boldly named Institute for the Future explains:

many social innovators err on the side of "ad-hocracy"—activating engagement without a carefully crafted "business plan," with roles and tasks emerging as the needs evolve. Instead of pursuing scale—investing in projects and initiatives that others can replicate and scale to multiple communities and populations (something of great concern to philanthropic institutions)—many social innovators take whatever limited resources they have to achieve impact where they perceive the highest need. Scale may result from networks of such individuals synchronizing actions, but it is often not their ultimate goal.

(Gorbis 2014)

Counter-intuitively, this giving-away of control over the end result of an initiative can create more significant impact. Henry Timms and Jeremy Heimans provide a neat example of this in their description of developing the #Giving-Tuesday hashtag: Timms' organisation, 92nd Street Y, developed the concept of a day of altruism, to encourage charitable donations after the buying frenzies of Black Friday and Cyber Monday (pre-Christmas sales days) (Heimans and Timms 2018:45). While 92nd Street Y set up a website and some basic tools to help any organisations that wanted to use the hashtag, they then allowed the online public to use the hashtag as they wished.

In its first year, 2015, the hashtag broke the world record for the amount of money raised in a single day on Giving Tuesday, but the real power behind this concept evolved over the next five years as it spread around the world and was adopted and, crucially, adapted. The hashtag was tweaked to become #Giving-BlueDay by the University of Michigan, it became #GivingShoesDay for the charity Dress for Success, it evolved into Giving Week in Singapore and #UnDiaParaDar in South America. This adaptability is a dimension that Timms and Heiman describe as 'extensible', meaning that others can extend the concept to fit their own circumstances. This extensibility does not involve permissions or branding discussions, and the more the original concept is used and adapted, the more powerful it becomes. Extensibility, though, does require the originating body, in this case 92nd Street Y, to cede control of its use and results in order for the concept to be successful. As Timms and Heiman say "it's only a movement if it moves without you" (Heimans and Timms 2018: 47).

Another powerful recent example of this, more diffuse, power was the mutual aid movement which sprang up in response the Covid-19 pandemic across the UK. Mutual aid groups were set up spontaneously by local residents, the groups were often attached to existing organisations (but not always charities). They were not restricted by specific requirements, as the Covid-19 Mutual Aid website sets out explicitly:

> Groups are not being set up in a uniform way and each community is advised to do what is best for them. These resources are here to give you some advice and pass on ways of working. These groups are not officially

affiliated with Covid-19 Mutual Aid UK and Covid-19 Mutual Aid UK is
not a (sic) official organisation.

(CovidMutualAid 2020)

This looseness of structure allowed for responses to be crafted to each local community's
assets and needs. It has also allowed for an agility and speed of response, which the New
Local Government Association's research describes as a counterpoint to more traditional
charities, which "cannot compete with the 'agility' of community groups, who have
been able to uncover need and get working almost immediately". Existing charities, the
research notes, were busy re-organising themselves during the chaotic early weeks of
the first national lockdown in 2020 (Tiratelli and Kaye 2020: 19).

A Conversation, Not a Broadcast

The mobilisation of an estimated 3 million people through 4,000 mutual aid
groups is a testament to the awe-inspiring potential power of engaging with a
wider community to make change happen (Tiratelli and Kaye 2020: 11). The
Giving Tuesday example illustrates well how the interconnectivity of the digital
world allows us access to resources and impact that we could not previously have
imagined. The most well-known example of this is Wikipedia.

From its very inception, in 2001, the Wikipedia website had a de-centralised
structure at its heart, in which the writing and editing of content is devolved to an
immense number of individual volunteer editors in many different languages. These
features enable the aggregation of the equivalent of thousands of volumes of the
Encyclopaedia Britannica, which are constantly updated and available to all, for free,
at the click of a mouse. The site is highly unusual in that it continues to be free of
charge to anyone to access and it refuses to take advertising revenue. It is a non-profit,
and secures external funding for its work. This type of open-sourced, crowd power is
also being harnessed for public good through other mass volunteering projects, like
the Missing Maps project, which gets volunteers to review satellite images and identify features that help disaster relief agencies who are often working in areas where
there are no accurate maps available.

A new generation of people (including volunteers and donors) are, however,
starting to expect more from their contacts with a charity than simply being given
tasks to do. Like the fundraisers online, who customised and re-imagined the
GivingTuesday concept, volunteers and donors who commit to a cause want to be
able to interact with it in some way, to have some agency or say in what the charity
does and how it does it. They are looking for feedback, connection and engagement
through their experience (RNLI 2019; Institute of Fundraising 2019a: 24). Digital
tools provide much more opportunity to do this. Increasingly people are able to
influence and engage with brands online, from websites where the audiences also
generate content, such as Reddit, to Instagram, where posts are greeted with real-
time feedback.

As this culture builds online there are increased expectations about how the charity sector interacts with its virtual audiences. As Reach Volunteering CEO Janet Thorne explained to me:

> It used to be OK, in fact it was accepted and approved of, that charities worked out of rubbish buildings. Our poor quality offices reflected how careful we were with our money. But today the shop window is our website and if you give people a poor experience online you'll just lose them.
>
> *(Thorne 2020)*

Charity service users and supporters have their tech expectations set by wealthy brands and there is a bleed-across into their expectations about the way charities present themselves and engage online (Institute of Fundraising 2019a: 14). After all, when other online interactions on Facebook or Twitter reward us with real-time feedback from a virtual community, it is only natural to expect that charities will respond to our offers of volunteering time or expertise instantaneously. Hearing nothing, or waiting a week for a response just isn't acceptable any longer (if indeed it ever was).

Some organisations have grasped with real enthusiasm the direct connection with the wider public, which the internet offers: fundraisers and campaigners have connected donors more directly with their cause; the campaigning website 38Degrees engages a crowd to campaign on specific issues, making it easy to take action on issues they care about. However, campaigns like this have also been accused of 'clicktivism', bringing about only superficial engagement of campaigners with the issues. Campaigning charities can though look to the models of organisations like Wikipedia or Reddit for ways to move their supporters from shallow, or passive support, to more active roles and devolved responsibility: Reddit superusers act as moderators for their groups and Wikipedia confers editor status on their more engaged content providers. The crowd brings expertise and resource, like a huge group of volunteers. But, like any volunteers, this crowd needs to be managed and engaged.

GiveDirectly, the US-based site, has taken a radically different approach to fundraising by funnelling donations directly to individual beneficiaries. This model is highly unusual, in that it does not fund local charitable projects on the ground in developing countries, but gives instead a cash payment direct to individuals in those regions. This takes further the concept of 'sponsorship' fundraising, which was popular in the 1990s (sponsoring a child's education in Africa, for example). Instead of paying towards the intermediary charity however, GiveDirectly places cash directly into the bank accounts of those in need. The organisation does not give out enormous amounts of money to any one individual, but its research demonstrates convincingly that these small, low bureaucracy, cash transfers do support people change their lives. Crucially, this process provides the recipients with agency – they, not an intermediary charity, decide how to spend the money they receive – and this is a small but important difference which enables people to retain their pride and independence.

Not a Charity Case

In his 1854 novel Walden, American philosopher Henry David Thoreau wrote:

> If I knew for a certainty that a man was coming to my house with the conscious design of doing me good, I should run for my life.
>
> *(Thoreau 1854: 71)*

This aversion to charity, alongside a recognition of the importance of self-esteem and agency, were recurrent themes in my interviews with charity sector leaders. As Banerjee and Duflo point out:

> The extreme poor are robbed of their dignity and their agency. They are made to understand that they should be grateful for help, even when they don't particularly want it. Robbed of their dignity, they easily become suspicious, and this suspicion is taken for ingratitude and obstinacy, which further deepens the trap in which they are stuck.
>
> *(Banerjee and Duflo 2019: 315)*

In their fascinating book, the economists explore the effectiveness of different approaches to poverty, and what is striking about the most effective programmes they review is the way that these are designed and iterated around the people it is supposed to help. This may sound like an obvious point, but so often we find interventions in the charity sector which conform to a standard model, or are based on someone's great idea, or on a small group of service users. These may well be interventions that worked at one time, or an a smaller scale, but which have not been iterated or adapted to a changing world.

One project examined by Banerjee and Duflo was the French employment organisation *Travailler et Apprendre Ensemble* ('Work and Learn Together'/ TAE). TAE challenged the accepted way of running unemployment projects, of 'giving' people jobs as a reward once they had jumped through various hoops. Instead they created communities of workers supporting one another, where the people themselves decide on the type of work they wanted to do and how they wanted to approach it. TAE was for the first time "asking people to contribute" to their own solutions (Banergee and Duflo 2019: 317).

This idea of engagement, the process of clearing away assumptions and listening to what people want and need, is really quite radical. Hillary Cottam's "open innovation" project, Circle, sought to enable older people to have "a flourishing third age" through engagement, and a dramatically different approach. For a start, the language was different. The very concept of the project was framed positively: instead of focusing on the challenges of ageing, it focused on older peoples' own capabilities, and on how to make ageing excellent:

> We suggested an innovation project that would start with older people themselves, that would include the abundance of experience and wealth and would ask how this could be shared in order to grow a new approach for all, rooted in prevention and the fostering of capabilities.
>
> *(Participle undated)*

This approach, Cottam notes, stands in marked contrast to many other charities supporting older people, where the focus is placed on the things which older people may *lack*; the needs that older people may have for services (needs, which only this particular charity claims they can help alleviate). Circle supported older people to form a community of mutual support, including people in their 50s and 60s as well as much older members. Crucially, the approach taken by Participle, Cottam's organisation, both here and in their other innovations, was to listen to what older people themselves wanted and to try out interventions that prevented them from falling into loneliness, or which helped them to continue to pursue hobbies or interests (Cottam 2018). This type of creative and personalised engagement, based on strong evidence, is exactly the sort of intervention that the charity sector should be well placed to develop.

Sometimes the last thing that someone needs is to feel like they are receiving charity. That is why many social enterprise organisations do not offer traditional charity support at all. The Magda Hotel in Vienna is a fascinating example of this. The Magda is:

> a social business that is not orientated around profit. Our aim is for people with a refugee background to get jobs and to give them training. And to make the world a better place together.
>
> *(Magda 2019)*

The hotel was set up by 20 former refugees and 18 hospitality professionals, and it responds to the chronic worklessness which many asylum seekers and refugees suffer. It also recognises, as Circle and TAE do, the assets of its people, explicitly referring to the "capabilities, talents, languages and cultural backgrounds" of refugees, which give them great potential as workers (ibid). The hotel has been an amazing success. As well as employing 20 recognised refugees and 13 trainees of 16 nationalities, with 20 languages spoken between them, the hotel is very popular – when I visited Vienna out of season in 2017 it was completely booked out.

This work speaks to a totally new power relationship between charities and beneficiaries – one in which the beneficiary gains some agency, their talents and abilities are fostered, and they are supported to gain their independence. This is also the essence of the approach taken by the Ashoka Foundation. This $26m endowment foundation invests directly in individuals it calls 'changemakers' through its Fellowship programme. It is agnostic about the type of organisation its Fellows are attached to, and it focuses primarily on the relational way in which they operate:

> Our Fellows address root causes of social problems to fundamentally disrupt those structures and change systems—they do this by creating new fields, building relationships where none previously existed, offering people new roles and relationships, and fundamentally helping people see differently so they can do differently.
>
> *(Ashoka 2019: 4)*

Complex Issues and Combined Solutions

The importance of engaging people in finding solutions is related to the complexity of the problems that face us today. With overwhelming issues like the climate crisis, it is not enough to wait for governments to take action and it is not enough just to do something as an individual, on our own. As the RED 'do-tank' puts it:

> most important modern problems are complex rather than complicated. Complex problems are messier and more ambiguous in nature; they are more connected to other problems; more likely to react in unpredictable non-linear ways; and more likely to produce unintended consequences. Tackling climate change is a good example: any solution would require many individuals and many global institutions to change behaviour on many different levels.
>
> *(Red 2006: 8)*

Collective impact provides a tantalising glimpse of a way to tackle some of these complex issues, without requiring each individual organisation to achieve an enormous increase in scale. This concept refers to initiatives that require a long-term commitment:

> by a group of important actors from different sectors to a common agenda for solving a specific social problem.
>
> *(Kania and Kramer 2011: 2)*

As the various actors involved coordinate their work around their shared objectives, this once again involves some ceding of control or ownership, as no single actor can claim responsibility for successful outcomes. Where the issues which a charity is attempting to tackle have many different strands, there is some evidence that this approach can bring about change where other "isolated impact" projects are not able to do so. In Cincinnati a charity called Strive brought together local actors to work together in tackling poor educational achievement across a wide geographical area. Over four years the collaborators saw improvements on key education indicators despite a recession and budget cuts (Kania and Kramer 2011).

Working on collective impact requires a different culture and approach from charities. It might be achieved in a range of different ways, including geographically specific, multi-stakeholder collaborations like Strive, but it could also be through, for example, a franchise model; or shared expertise, such as Alcoholics Anonymous's resource-centre approach (Gugelev and Stern 2015). Key to each of these models is the idea that no one single actor needs to be everywhere or to do everything, but instead should draw on the complementary assets of other actors – their local reach, their credibility with certain audiences, their ability to capture and analyse data – in order to achieve shared goals. Through these collective approaches, which focus relentlessly on a common objective, charities have the potential to extend their impact and achieve the scale commensurate with their ambition.

If at First You Don't Succeed…

One of the fascinating aspects of Hillary Cottam's Participle organisation is its learning from failure. She is very open about the challenges they faced and the aspects of Circle which led to its London programme closing. Reading about what did *not* work in Participle's trialled interventions is incredibly refreshing. Cottam not only sets out what did not work, but she is also genuinely interested in exploring why. She recognises that it is the failures in some of their projects which lead them to a better understanding of what works, and why.

This process of quickly reviewing, assessing and then changing an intervention is common in the business world, popularised by lean management techniques, but it has not filtered into the charity world. It is unsurprising to see this approach being used in the experimental Participle projects, but we can also see it in action in the development of the Extinction Rebellion (XR) movement. XR is controversial in its methods, but it is useful to examine it here because, whatever one thinks of its work, it has adopted an interesting approach. The way in which it has adapted offers some useful insights into how new ways of working can be harnessed for different causes.

XR ran a series of campaigns to raise awareness of the climate crisis and push for action in April 2019, which resulted in the UK government and numerous councils declaring a climate crisis (Taylor 2020). However, the organisation wanted to effect much more significant change, so it was constantly re-evaluating what works in order to better target its resources for impact. XR wanted to put more pressure on decision-makers, whom it felt had made big promises but had not taken action. It also wanted to be more agile and responsive to its activists on the ground, to make better use of their intelligence to inform decisions about where to move demonstrations. So when XR returned in the autumn of 2019 it had evolved its approach.

Unlike many campaigning non-profit organisations, XR does not have a cen-tralised structure which dictates to its supporters what to say, what to do and how to do it. Nor does it operate as a complete democracy, with the challenges of agreeing every single decision through a slow committee and discussion process. Instead XR has started to use elements of the relatively new (self)-management structure known as holacracy, which aims to balance power across an organisa-tion, while still enabling some actors greater decision-making agency than others. It aims to enable speedier learning and the agile development of responses to a rapidly changing context (Holocracy 2020). This structure has enabled XR to be extremely adaptable. Its activists now operate in a series of circles or cells, which operate independently, but within the core principles of XR in what the *Econo-mist* refers to as being "in effect franchises of the main brand" (The Economist 2019). This structure allows XR to draw on the creativity of its activists, also, crucially, it gives its activists a sense of agency. They develop their own activities and deliver these themselves, resulting in numerous, and highly original, cam-paigning stunts. The downside of this lack of control though is that it can result in poorly judged initiatives, such as the protest at Shadwell tube in 2019 which drew criticism for attacking public transport infrastructure, a key alternative to highly polluting forms of private transport (Townsend 2019).

In addition to changing their organisational structure, XR has shown a will-ingness to pick and mix the technologies it uses to meet its changing needs, using Signal and MatterMost for internal communications and Telegram for a more effective feedback loop for those on the site of demonstrations. In doing so it has shown what Alex Hensby at the University of Kent has described as 'tactical flexibility', learning quickly from its experience (Kobie 2019). It is a characteristic of today's successful for-profit companies that they are also constantly learning. The availability of data about our interactions with companies enables learning and this data will only become deeper and richer over time.

Companies today are able to map their customer journeys and to trial tweaks to their customer interface, comparing effectiveness immediately and using that data to continuously improve their products. Netflix is an interesting example of this. Unlike many other web-based companies, like Facebook, Netflix does not rely on advertising for income. While the company may not be gathering user data for advertisers, it does gather enormous amounts of data about its viewers, to help it to understand what they prefer to watch, when and how. This intelligence then shapes Netflix's decisions on programming (Leslie 2020). Unlike the feedback loops of the voluntary sector, which remain ossified in the form of surveys and direct questions, feedback in the digital age is based on directly observed behaviour, often without us even being aware of it. If Netflix were a charity, it would probably have asked me to fill out a survey on my favourite shows and then stored my responses in a lever arch file to be shared at the end of the year with its investors.

This, and many of the other examples here may sound a million miles away from the charities you know and love, but they really are not. And, in a world that is moving very quickly around us, they should not be. The Covid-19 crisis is already accelerating our digital development at a faster rate than any of us might have expected in 2019. By the time you read this book I expect that some of the examples I have given here will already be out of date, but the principle behind them will not be: there are always new and emerging ways of engaging with charities' service users and their supporters, and there are new ways for non-profits to be organised and run. Charities should have the freedom to look around at what others in their own sector and beyond are doing, and have the flexibility to develop and design their services differently. This is partly a cultural change within the sector, but it does also require a change in attitudes from external stakeholders to free up charities to pursue a new course.

9

CAN CHARITIES CHANGE THE WORLD?

Charities as they exist in 2021 are hugely varied, but expectations about what charities do and the way that they do this are not. In the public imagination and in the culture of many charities there is a persistent idea of charities as paragons of virtue, able to produce miraculous results through sacrifice and commitment. This defining set of expectations is holding back the charities that do want to tackle major social and environmental issues. By mythologising the charity culture of frugality and sacrifice for a cause, and by underestimating the planning, coordination and skill that goes into running successful charities, we drastically under-value the skills of charity leaders and the importance of investing in charity infrastructure.

These expectations about charities are mutually contradictory: we want charities to be set up by inspired individuals on a voluntary basis, but we also want these individuals to address areas of benefit to the general public. We want donors to give generously to charitable causes because they feel an emotional connection with the charity, but then donors ask the charity to report on their actual impact. We pressure charities to diversify their funding, but then get frustrated with them for spending too much time and money on fundraising, and not enough on their service users. We want charities to show they are making a difference, but we will not pay for the systems and people they need to do this. We want charities to be more professional, but we also want to see them offer lower salaries and rely more on the use of volunteers. We want charities to be more efficient, but we expect them to run on a shoestring.

When one traces a route through the real experiences of people leading charities today, as we have done in this book, it is possible to see that, while each of these expectations on its own can seem valid and understandable, taken as a whole they weave into an overwhelming and complex web in which charities have become ensnared. It is then no surprise that the charity sector today is suffering from stagnation.

DOI: 10.4324/9781003139089-9

Today's charities operate in a world which is more complex than ever before, and which is changing at a gathering pace. In order to support charities to navigate this world successfully it is important that we, the public, and charities themselves, are clear and realistic about what we expect charities to achieve. Do we want all charities to be localised expressions of personal altruism, or do we want some charities to lead on social and environmental change, to innovate and to realise economies of scale? Do we want, and need, charities to operate as paragon-organisations with best-in-class terms and conditions for employees, with strong records in diversity and inclusion, and with impressive environmental credentials? And if so, are we prepared to pay for this?

Charities have enormous potential to tackle the issues we face today. Their cohesive sense of mission acts as a kind of adrenaline to their employees, inspiring staff to work harder, and for longer hours for less pay than in other professions. Talented people increasingly want to work for organisations that fit with their values and make a difference to society. Technology is enabling more and more of the sort of volunteering and collaboration opportunities that have been at the heart of the charity sector since its inception. Charities' ability to reach and involve wider groups of stakeholders is precisely the direction of travel of modern movements and organisations, and this is exactly the sort of reach that is crucial in combatting social division and overcoming inequality. And, in a world where the general public has less and less faith in the ability of institutions to solve problems, there is a gap which trusted charities could, and should, fill.

It is often forgotten that the father of the welfare state, William Beveridge, concluded that even where a strong state exists, there was an important and enduring role for charities, both as innovators piloting new solutions to social issues, and as services able to meet unmet needs. Charities are needed "to do things that the state 'should not do' or was 'most unlikely' to do" (Beveridge 1948). However, as one former charity CEO said, echoing the frustrations of many I spoke with for this book "[Charities] actually punch way below our weight, despite what we tell ourselves" (Interviewee S 2020). Charities just are not set up in a way that enables them to tackle new and emerging problems, and to do so at scale and at pace. As Jenny North, Director of Policy at the social investment foundation, Impetus PEF, points out:

> Driven largely by visibility and advertising what we have is a super- league of charities that is so static. During a recession we should expect new entrants coming into this space. That this doesn't happen is a sign of a dysfunctional sector. Instead, charities with brilliant solutions to seemingly intractable social problems don't get the chance to scale up and get bigger and reach more people. There isn't any evidence that funding is flowing to the organisations with the best track record of improving outcomes, or with the most potential to do this in the future.
>
> *(Centre for Social Justice 2013: 15)*

So, new charities are not driving innovation at the scale needed, and there are not the incentives to push large charities, North's 'static' 'super-league', to innovate either. The way in which charities are funded directs them away from learning and collaboration and genuine innovation. Also, as we have seen, the funding does not follow the issues of greatest social need. Part-time, volunteer trustees may work well for small, community-focused charities, but their lack of attention or skills, or lack of experience at a strategic level, can hold back the development and growth of ambitious charities. Crucially, the way that we expect all charities to operate on a shoestring seriously impedes innovation and forward-planning.

All the areas of challenge we have examined in this book contribute to the inertia we see in charities today and this presents a serious threat to charities' sustainability. In their 2020 survey NPC unearthed an interesting contradiction: when they asked charities about their plans for the immediate future (prior to the Covid-19 pandemic) they found that:

> charities were doing *more of everything we asked about in 2017* and planned to do even more in the future. This came despite overall funding for the sector remaining relatively static, which suggests that charities were already stretching their resources before the crisis.
>
> *(NPC 2020: 4) (my italics)*

This reflects the difficulty that charities experience in trying to imagine a different future, and their tendency to drift into spreading themselves too thin by simply trying to do more with limited resources and with funding that does not cover costs. It also underlines charities' tendency to focus on business-as-usual. Charities rarely have the opportunity to take stock of their work, to re-evaluate and re-plan, because the complex interaction of their funding and projects and stakeholders makes it incredibly difficult to pause the tanker that is their business-as-usual, let alone to turn that tanker around.

The social, economic and technological changes we are living through, however, just will not allow for this level of stasis. Charities today need to be thinking above all about their charitable mission, and they need to creatively re-imagine how they deliver this for the service users of the future in very different ways. In the coming decades, the Fourth Industrial Revolution, as the World Economic Forum describes it, will profoundly change not just how we work, but what we do and why we do it:

> [The Fourth Industrial Revolution] will accelerate the introduction of game-changing technologies that will further empower consumers and enable once-impossible business models. The ability to respond to changing needs of the marketplace will be key to future success and implies material changes to the way companies operate. Businesses must re-invent themselves by establishing an agile and enduring enterprise in a highly disruptive world while also ensuring inclusive societies.
>
> *(World Economic Forum 2018)*

What goes for businesses also holds true for charities. As we have seen, the boundaries between non-profit and for-profit enterprises are more fluid online. Consumers' expectations will be set by their online interactions with for-profits and will bleed across into their expectations of charities. The Institute of Fundraising recognises this shift and the fact that charities are lagging behind:

> Consumers want organisations to understand them, to meet/pre-empt their needs, to listen to them and to respond accordingly. The general feeling was that charities have struggled to keep up with this and the gap between expectation and reality is widening rather than closing
>
> *(Institute of Fundraising 2019a: 14).*

Throughout this book it has been a constant challenge to address the hugely varying aims and needs of the wide variety of organisations bundled together under the title 'charity'. Almost everything one can say about the sector as a whole has to come with a caveat – what impedes the work of one size or type of charity may function perfectly for another. The very expansiveness of the definition of charity seems to be one element which holds back the sector, because public expectations are shaped by one variant of charity (for example the small, community-based, volunteer-led football club) and then confounded by another (a multi-million-pound regional care provider).

In response to this heterogeneity academics and think-tanks have suggested bundling charities differently, segmenting them by type or size, and treating them differently. Whatever the size or focus of the charity however, there is one defining aspect of the organisation which will determine how they need to be regarded or regulated. That is – what is the charity for? Is charity an expression of emotion and caring – that is to say, providing relief, support or a sense of community, set up as an expression of the founder's passion for a cause – or does it aim to fix things, to change the world and solve problems?

In my view, these are two very different types of organisation and too often charities are trying to do both or masquerading as one when, in fact, they are the other. Charities that are set up to fundraise for a cause which a founder feels passionately about, and which their individual donors also feel an emotional attachment to, should not be forced into the straitjacket of complex impact measurement if they are not really trying to change anything. Conversely, charities which are developing innovative solutions to emerging problems absolutely need to be able to demonstrate their path to impact, but should not be constrained by traditional views about frugality and reserve levels, which could stymie their accumulation of working capital and ability to hire the specialist staff they need.

By trying to pretend to be one sort of organisation, when they are the other, risks eroding public trust in charities and fosters unrealistic expectations. An increasing emphasis on transparency and engagement in public discourse will require charities to be clearer about what they are for, and how they are making a difference. The public, including donors and supporters, will expect charities to be straight with them about projects which do not work, about what they spend and why.

For those charities that do want to solve problems and to tackle emerging issues there are some important new opportunities emerging. But in order to take advantage of new ways of working and the opportunity to develop new services, charities need more freedom in the way that they operate.

These charities need to be able to find time and resource to look up from the day-to-day, and to really challenge themselves about the future. Charities, like businesses, need to take the future seriously and prepare for it, investing in horizon-scanning and in research and development. Charities need the resource and the space to develop and pilot initiatives and to learn from these. RNLI for instance has a whole innovation team, and has shared its own thinking on this in its Innovate Blog and through a blog for Charities Aid Foundation. An established charity with healthy levels of income, RNLI is thinking ahead, scanning the future for opportunities and challenges and, generously, also sharing some of its insights with the rest of the sector. It should not be the reserve only of the very wealthy charities like RNLI to innovate like this.

The emphasis on innovation, though, may not be enough. As Starr and Coussa point out, innovation is pointless if it never gets adopted widely:

> the most urgent challenge in the social sector is not innovation, but replication. No idea will drive big impact at scale unless organizations—a lot of them—replicate it. And there are plenty of high-impact ideas awaiting high-quality replication. More than a few of them are backed by randomized controlled trial (RCT) results and all that stuff. It turns out that replication matters even more than innovation when it comes to impact at scale.
>
> *(Starr and Coussa 2018)*

They also go on to emphasise that it is smaller-scale social ventures, rather than large NGOs, which drive innovation in the international development field, through their agility and focus. In the private sector these innovators would be bought up by larger companies and developed and scaled. Perhaps there is an opportunity for charities to think in this way too, and for the sector to innovate through acquisition?

However, as we have seen throughout this book, charities' ability to take bold steps like this, to redefine their purpose and to anticipate and prepare for the future is continually hampered. Charities face barriers on a number of fronts: through the limitations of part-time and voluntary trustees; through the confines of restricted funding; lack of skilled staff and the myriad claims on charities' time which yield little in terms of their mission. Charities can be held back by onerous and duplicative separate impact reporting requirements; by dealing with sniping about salary levels and hand-wringing about the latest 'scandal'. Other ties binding charities' hands are less visible but no less restrictive: the culture of sacrifice which runs charity infrastructure down to its metal, which suppresses staff salaries, scrimps on training and support, undermines trading, and which bears down on the reserves that could be built up into working capital to fund research and development.

With these hurdles facing charities it is fair to ask, as several of my interviewees did, whether, if we were trying to tackle social problems today, would we do so through the framework of a registered charity?

The boundaries between charities and businesses are becoming more blurred. For many years the press has recognised a growing convergence between the sectors as charities become more businesslike. With a growing acceptance of "conscious consumerism" businesses are also now channelling charities by defining their social or environmental purpose, by tracking their social and environmental impact and by taking up traditionally charitable activities, such as campaigning (Grattan 2018). New organisations are set up, as companies or social enterprises, to tackle issues which might once have been charities' domain. As one interviewee for Charity Benchmarking Report put it:

> The space for charities is closing. People increasingly don't see a distinction between charity, social enterprises and corporates doing good. Those charities that don't adapt will get lost; they'll lose their relevance.
>
> *(Institute of Fundraising 2019a: 16)*

It makes sense for new problem-solving organisations to take on whatever form (business, social enterprise, social movement or charity) best enables them to achieve their mission. Whether charities continue to be a preferred form for this venture depends on whether we can develop our thinking about what the future charity can and should be. I hope, and believe, that charities can liberate themselves from the stranglehold of expectations and tradition that binds them. I hope that this book can at least offer some initial thoughts on this, and that it may prompt discussion to help re-imagine the sector for the decades ahead, where charities' insights, their reach and their tenacity will be needed more than ever.

BIBLIOGRAPHY

ACEVO (2018) Racial Diversity in the Charity Sector, *ACEVO*, July 2018.

ACF (2019) *Foundation Giving Trends 2019*, Association of Charitable Foundations.

Ainsworth, D. (2018) Why the Daily Mail Got It Wrong on RNLI, *Civil Society* website, 14 May 2018.

Ainsworth, D. (2020) *Made to Measure? How Should Charities Assess Effectiveness?* Charity Awards 2020 website, *Civil Society Media*, accessed 21 November 2020.

Alcock, P. (2010) A Strategic Unity: Defining the Third Sector in the UK. *Voluntary Sector Review*, 1(1), pp.5–24.

Alcock, P., Butt, C. and Macmillan, R. (2013) *Unity in Diversity: What is the Future for the Third Sector?*Third Sector Futures Dialogue 2012–2013. Third Sector Research Centre.

Ashoka (2019) *Impact Report 2019*, The Ashoka Foundation.

Atkinson, M. (2018) *Guest Blog: Mark Atkinson: Being Bold Has Paid Off for Scope, Social Club UK* website, 6 April 2018.

Atkinson, M. (2019) *Interviewed Mitchell, S.* (16 December 2019).

Bailey, D. and Kerlin, L. (2015) Can Health Trainers Make A Difference With Difficult-To-Engage Clients? A Multisite Case Study, *Health Promotion Practice*, 16(5), pp.756–764.

Banergee, A.V. and Duflo, E. (2019) *Good Economics For Hard Times: Better Answers To Our Biggest Problems*, Penguin UK.

Banjoko, T. (2020) *Interviewed Mitchell, S.* (25 June 2020).

Barnardo's (2019) *Working With Barnardo's, Barnardo's Corporate Strategy Refresh*.

Barnardo's (2020) *Barnardo's Mission Statement, Barnardo's* website, accessed November 2020.

Bateman, A. (2020) *Interviewed Mitchell, S.* (5 June 2020).

BBC (2019) *Lloyds Reveals Depths Of Sexual Harassment Culture, BBC* website, 24 September 2019.

BBC (2020) *Amazon Pays £290m In UK Tax As Sales Surge To £14bn, BBC* website, 9 September 2020.

Beveridge, V.A. (1948) *A Report on Methods of Social Advance*, Voluntary Action.

Blake, J. (2020) *Interviewed Mitchell, S.* (10 February 2020).

Breeze, B. (2013) *How Donors Choose Charities: The Role Of Personal Taste and Experiences in Giving Decisions, Voluntary Sector Review*, 4(2), pp.165–183.

Brignall, M. (2016) Age UK Criticised Over E.ON Partnership, *The Guardian*, 19 April 2016.

Brindle, D. (2020) *Regulator's Warning To Avoid Culture Wars Only Increases Strained Relations With Charities, The Guardian*, 30 November 2020.

Bryson, J.R., McGuiness, M. and Ford, R.G.(2002) Chasing a 'Loose and Baggy Monster': Almshouses and the Geography Of Charity. *Area*, 34(1), pp.48–58.

Bubb, S. (2017) *The History of British Charity*, lecture delivered at New College, Oxford.

Burne James, S. (2015) *Charity Commission Removes Almost 1,000 Charities in 'Register Cleanse', Third Sector*, 30 January 2015.

CAF (2019) *CAF UK Giving 2019*, Charities Aid Foundation.

CAF (2020) *Three Months Into Lockdown, How Are Charities In The UK Faring?* Charities Aid Foundation Charity Coronavirus Briefing, June 2020.

Cancer Research UK (2019) *Annual Report and Accounts Cancer Research UK 2018–19*, Cancer Research UK.

Caplin, J. (2019) It's Time, *Barnardo's* blog, Barnardo's website, 8 February 2019.

Carnegie, A. (1889) The Best Fields For Philanthropy, *The North American Review*, 149 (397), pp.682–698.

Cass Business School (undated.a) *The True and Fair Foundation report 'A Hornet's Nest: A Review of Charitable Spending by UK Charities' Cass Centre for Charity Effectiveness Responds*, Cass Centre for Charity Effectiveness.

Cass Business School (undated.b) *Cost Recovery Tools For Success: Doing The Right Things And Doing Them Well*, Cass Centre for Charity Effectiveness.

Centre for Social Justice (2013) *Something's Got To Give: The State of Britain's Voluntary and Community Sector*, Centre for Social Justice.

Charity Commission (2013) *Charitable Purpose (Guidance)*, The Charity Commission.

Charity Commission (2018) *The Essential Trustee*, The Charity Commission.

Charity Commission (2019) *Charity Commission Annual Report and Accounts 2018–19* (For the year ended 31 March 2019).

Charity Commission et al. (2017) *Taken on Trust: The Awareness and Effectiveness of Charity Trustees in England And Wales*, Charity Commission et al, November 2017.

Charity Retail Association (2020) Charity Retail Association website FAQs, accessed September 2020.

Civil Exchange (2015) Whose Society? The Big Society Audit, *Civil Exchange*, January 2015.

Clark, D. (2021) Charities With the Most Employees in England and Wales 2021, *Statistica website,* 8 January 2021.

Clic Sargent (2019) Clic Sargent Publishes Its Annual Impact and Accountability Report – the Good, the Bad and the Ugly, Clic Sargent website, 29 November 2019.

Clifford, D. (2017) Charitable Organisations, The Great Recession and the Age of Austerity: Longitudinal Evidence for England and Wales, *Journal of Social Policy*, 46(1), pp.1–30.

Clore (2016a) Leadership Development in the Third Sector: Learning Lessons, *Clore Social Leadership*.

Clore (2016b) Leadership Development in the Third Sector: Bridging Supply and Demand, *Clore Social Leadership*.

Comic Relief (2020) Where Your Donation Goes, *Comic Relief* website, 3 October 2020.

Community Care (2015) The Sudden Death Of BAAF: How It Happened And What It May Mean For Social Work, *Community Care*, 13 August 2015.

Cone (2016) *Cone Communications Millennial Employment Engagement Survey 2016*, Cone.

Cooney, R. (2019) Charities 'Woeful' On Diversity For Disabled People, Says Arts Council Chief, *Third Sector*, 3 July 2019.

Cooney, R. (2020) *Cancer Research UK to Cut Almost a Quarter of Its Workforce*, *Third Sector*, 15 July 2020.

Cordery, C.J., Smith, K.A. and Berger, H. (2017) Future Scenarios For the Charity Sector in 2045, *Public Money & Management*, 37(3), pp.189–196.

Corry, D. (2014) *How Do We Drive Productivity And Innovation In The Charity Sector?*, RSA Lecture, 8 May 2014.

Corry, D. (2020a) Where Are England's Charities?, *New Philanthropy Capital*, January 2020.

Corry, D. (2020) *Interviewed Mitchell, S.* (10 March 2020).

Cottam, H. (2018) *Radical Help: How We Can Remake the Relationships Between Us and Revolutionise the Welfare State*, Hachette.

CovidMutualAid (2020) Local Group Resources, *CovidMutualAid* website (accessed December 2020).

Crisis (2021) Everybody In: How To End Homelessness In Great Britain, *Crisis* website, 20 March 2021.

Davies, R. (2016) *Public Good By Private Means: How Philanthropy Shapes Britain*, Alliance Publishing Trust.

de Grunwald, T. (2011) Are Charity Interns Really Volunteers? *The Guardian* online, 28 June 2011.

Dees, J.G. (2012). A Tale Of Two Cultures: Charity, Problem Solving, and the Future of Social Entrepreneurship, *Journal of Business Ethics*, 111(3), pp.321–334.

Degli Antoni, G. (2009) Intrinsic Vs. Extrinsic Motivations To Volunteer And Social Capital Formation, *Kyklos*, 62(3), pp.359–370.

Dickens, C. (1853) *Bleak House*, Penguin, 1971.

Economist (2019) How the Anarchists of Extinction Rebellion Got So Well Organised, *The Economist*, 10 October 2019.

Equality Trust (2021) About Us, *Equality Trust* website, 20 March 2021.

Eton (2020) Our History, *Eton College* website, accessed 15 December 2020.

Fiennes, C. (2013) Good Charities Spend More on Administration Than Less Good Charities Spend, *Giving Evidence* website, 2 May, pp.2–13.

Fiennes, C. (2016) How Can We Make Impact Measurement More Useful?, *Civil Society*, 15 November 2016.

Financial Times (2017) Kids Company Trustees Face Bans From Running UK Companies, *Financial Times*, 31 July 2017.

Fitzpatrick, R. and Thorne, L. (2019) *In Plain Sight: Workplace Bullying in Charities and the Implications for Leadership*, Centre for Mental Health, June 2019.

Gatenby Sanderson (undated) *Thriving in an Age of Disruption: How Leaders Are Adapting For the Future*, Gatenby Sanderson.

Getting On Board (2017) *The Looming Crisis in Charity Trustee Recruitment: How Poor Trustee Recruitment Practices Threaten to Damage The Effectiveness of UK Charities*, Getting on Board.

Gissing, G. (1889) *The Nether World*, Oxford World's Classics, 2008.

Glenn, K. (2020) *Interviewed Mitchell, S.* (28 May 2020).

Golightly, M. and Holloway, M. (2016) Editorial, *The British Journal of Social Work*, 46(1), January 2016, pp.1–7.

Gorbis, M. (2014) Second Curve Philanthropy, *Stanford Social Innovation Review*, 1 December 2014.

Grant, M. (2020) *Interviewed Mitchell, S.* (1 February 2020).

Grattan, E. (2018) Conscious Consumerism: What It Means, Why It's Popular and Why It's Changing the World, *Triodos Bank* website.

Green, F., Anders, J., Henderson, M. and Henseke, G. (2017) *Who Chooses Private Schooling In Britain And Why* (LLAKES Research Paper 62).

Gugelev, A. and Stern, A. (2015) What's Your Endgame, *Stanford Social Innovation Review*, 13(1), pp.40–47.

Gunn, M.R. (2020) *Interviewed Mitchell, S.* (16 January 2020).

Harries, R. (2016) *Leadership Development in the Third Sector: Bridging Supply and Demand*, Clore Social Leadership.

Harris, E. (2019) The Louvre Took Down the Sackler Name. Here's Why Other Museums Probably Won't, *New York Times*, 18 July 2019.

Heimans, J. and Timms, H. (2018) *New Power: Why Outsiders Are Winning, Institutions Are Failing, And How The Rest Of Us Can Keep Up In The Age Of Mass Participation*. Pan Macmillan.

Hill, M. (2020) *Interviewed Mitchell, S.* (23 June 2020).

Hind, A. (2011) New Development: Increasing Public Trust and Confidence In Charities: On The Side of the Angels, *Public Money & Management*, 31(3), pp.201–205.

HM Treasury (2020) Chancellor Sets Out Extra £750 Million Coronavirus Funding For Frontline Charities, HM Treasury press release, 8 April 2020.

Hodges, J. and Howieson, B. (2017) The Challenges Of Leadership in the Third Sector, *European Management Journal*, 35(1), pp.69–77.

Hoffman, K. (2013) Escaping The Prisoner's Dilemma: Understanding The UK's Charity Sector's Ability To Do Its Best And Do Good, *Philanthropy Impact*, Spring.

Holocracy (2020) Why Practice Holocracy?, *The Holocracy.org* website, accessed December 2020.

House of Commons (2016) *The Collapse Of Kids Company: Lessons For Charity Trustees, Professional Firms*, the Charity Commission, and Whitehall, House of Commons Public Administration and Constitutional Affairs Committee, Report of Session 2015–2016.

House of Lords (2017) Stronger Charities For A Stronger Society, *House of Lords Select Committee on Charities, Report of Session 2016–2017*, House of Lords Paper 133.

Housman, C. (2020) *Interviewed Mitchell, S.* (29 May 2020).

Hurst, G. (2020) Charities Rebuked As Complaints About Street Collectors Rise, *The Times*, 5 September 2020.

Hwang, H. and Powell, W.W. (2009) The Rationalization Of Charity: The Influences of Professionalism in the Nonprofit Sector, *Administrative Science Quarterly*, 54(2), pp.268–298.

Hyndman, N. (2017) The Charity Sector—Changing Times, Changing Challenges, *Public Money and Management*, 37(3), pp.149–153.

Institute of Fundraising (2019a) *Charity Benchmarks Sector Report*, Institute of Fundraising.

Institute of Fundraising (2019b) *Year in Fundraising 2019*, Institute of Fundraising.

Interviewee S (2020) *Interviewed Mitchell, S.* (June 2020).

Interviewee T (2020) *Interviewed Mitchell, S.* (May 2020)

Interviewee U (2020) *Interviewed Mitchell S.* (June 2020).

Interviewee V (2020) *Interviewed Mitchell, S.* (May 2020).

Interviewee W (2020) *Interviewed Mitchell, S.* (June 2020).

Jordan, W.K. (2016) *Philanthropy in England*, Routledge.

Kania, J. and Kramer, M. (2011) Collective Impact, *Stanford Social Innovation Review*, Winter 2011, pp.36–41.

Kay, L. (2018) Three in 10 RSPCA Staff Say they Have Been Bullied in the Past Year, *Third Sector*, 22 October 2018.

Kay, L. (2019) Most Charity Workers are Stressed at Work Unite Survey Finds, *Third Sector*, 20 May 2019.

Kay, L. (2020) Scope Income Falls by £40m After Sell-Off of Services, *Civil Society*, 6 January 2020.

Keogh, G. and Braithwaite, S. (2019) Charity Bosses' Five-Figure Rises Revealed, *Daily Mail* online, 24 August 2019.

Khan, J. (2018) Strategic Partnerships Are the Way Ahead, *Third Sector*, 29 October 2018.

Kids Company and the Company Directors Disqualification Act (2021) *In The Matter of Keeping Kids Company And In The Matter Of The Company Directors Disqualification Act 1986*, Case no: CR-2017-006113, Mrs Justice Falk, The High Court of Justice Business and Property Courts of England and Wales Insolvency and Companies List (ChD), 12 February 2021.

Kobie, N. (2019) How Extinction Rebellion Evolved Its Tactics for Its London Protests, *Wired*, 7 October 2019.

Kruger, D. (2020) *Levelling Up Our Communities: A Proposal For A New Social Contract*, September 2020.

Leslie, I. (2020) How Netflix Changed The Channel, *New Statesman*, 10 December 2020.

Liao-Troth, M.A. (2005) Are They Here for the Long Haul? The Effects of Functional Motives and Personality Factors on the Psychological Contracts of Volunteers, *Nonprofit and Voluntary Sector Quarterly*, 34(4), pp.510–530.

Lien, C., Katerji, A. and Griffiths, S. (2020) *Interviewed Mitchell, S.* (14 November 2020).

Linklaters (2018) Linklaters Recognised for Outstanding Pro Bono Contribution to the International Bar Association eyeWitness Project, *Linklaters* website, 8 October 2018.

Living Wage Foundation (2017) Low Pay in the Charity Sector Report 2017, *Living Wage Foundation*.

Lloyds Bank Foundation (2016) *Commissioning in Crisis*, Lloyd's Bank Foundation of England and Wales, December 2016.

Lloyds Bank Foundation and NCVO (2013) *Financial Trends For Small to Medium Sized Charities*, Lloyds Bank Foundation and NCVO.

MacAskill, W. (2015) *Doing Good Better: Effective Altruism And A Radical New Way To Make A Difference*, Guardian Faber Publishing.

Magdo (2019) *Magdas Konzept*, promotional flyer downloaded from the Magda Hotel website, 2019.

Magor, J. (2019) *ESG Investors Need A Single Standard To Measure Impact, Reuters Events*, 26 June 2019.

Massive/Kivo Future Charity (2019) *The Future Charity, How To Drive Change And Innovation Across The Sector*.

McGrath, H. (2020) *Interviewed Mitchell, S.* (10 January 2020).

McLeod, R. and Clay, T. (2018) Make It Count: Why Impact Matters in User Involvement, *New Philanthropy Capital*.

Miller, C. (2003) Hidden In Plain Sight, *Non-Profit Quarterly*.

Miller, C. (2005) *The Looking-Glass World Of Nonprofit Money: Managing In For-Profits' Shadow Universe, The Nonprofit Quarterly*, 12(1), pp.48–55.

Montecute, R. (2018) *Internships 2018 Briefing*, Sutton Trust.

Morris, S. (2016) Poppy Seller Who Killed Herself Got 3,000 Charity Requests For Donations a Year, *The Guardian*, 20 January 2016.

Muslim Aid (2018) *Mind The Gap: A Review Of The Voluntary Sector Response To The Grenfell Tragedy, Muslim Aid*, May 2018.

National Audit Office (2013) *The Regulatory Effectiveness Of The Charity Commission*, Report by the Comptroller and the Auditor General, HC 813 Session 2013–14, 4 December 2013.

NCVO (2004) *Standing Apart, Working Together A Study Of The Myths And Realities Of Voluntary And Community Sector Independence*, NCVO, 2004.

NCVO (2014a) *Report of the Inquiry Into Charity Senior Executive Pay and Guidance For Trustees on Setting Remuneration*, NCVO, April 2014.

NCVO (2014b) *Payment By Results And The Voluntary Sector*, NCVO, April 2014.

NCVO (2018) Britain's Biggest Charities: Key Features, *NCVO Research Briefing*, November 2018.

NCVO (2019a) *Civil Society Almanac 2019*, NCVO.

NCVO (2019b) *Time Well Spent*, NCVO, January 2019.

NCVO (2020) *Civil Society Almanac*, NCVO.

Never More Needed (2020) Charities Are Facing a £12.4bn Shortfall in Income for the Year Due to Impact Of Coronavirus, *Never More Needed* website, 19 June 2020.

Nichols, G. (2013) The Psychological Contract of Volunteers: A New Research Agenda, *Voluntas: International Journal of Voluntary & Nonprofit Organizations*, 24(4), p.986.

NPC (2020) *State of the Sector 2020, New Philanthropy Capital*, 18 May.

Osula, B. and Ng, E.C. (2014) Toward A Collaborative, Transformative Model Of Non-Profit Leadership: Some Conceptual Building Blocks, *Administrative Sciences*, 4(2), pp.87–104.

Owen, R. (2017) Our Pioneering Project Has Cut Reoffending - and Paid a 3% Dividend, *The Guardian* website, 9 August 2013.

Oxfam (2019) *Oxfam Annual Report and Accounts 2018–19*.

Palmer, A. (2020) What The EU's Investigation Of Amazon Means For U.S. Antitrust Probes, CNBC website, *CNBC* website, 11 November 2020.

Participle (undated) Ageing>Circle, *Participle* website, accessed 20 March 2021.

Penna, D. (2020) Aid Charities Admit They are Not Doing Enough to Stop Volunteers Sexually Exploiting Vulnerable People, *The Telegraph*, 21 October 2020.

Pomroy, B. (2020) *Interviewed Mitchell, S.* (1 June 2020).

Populus and Charity Commission (2018) *Trust in Charities, 2018: How The Public Views Charities, What This Means For The Sector, And How Trust Can Be Increased*, July 2018, Populus and The Charity Commission.

Pudelek, J. (2013) Too Many 'Careerists' in the Voluntary Sector, Says Philanthropist, *Third Sector*, 06 March 2013.

Purkis, A. (2020) *Are Charitable Services Essential?, Civil Society*, 16 April 2020.

Radojev, H. (2016) Charity Brand Index Finds That No Charities Improved Score in 2015, *Civil Society News*, 29 January 2016.

Radojev, H. (2018) *Charities 'Taking Chunks Out Of Each Other' To Raise Funds*, Civil Society, 18 October 2018.

Red (2006) *Red Paper 02: Transformational Design*, Burns, C., Cottam, H., Vanstone, C., Winhall, J., Design Council.

Reynolds, M. (2017) If You Can't Build It, Buy It: Google's Biggest Acquisitions Mapped, *Wired*, 25 November 2017.

RNLI (2019) *Futures 2050*, Wilson, M., Eaton, M., RNLI slide deck.

Rose-Ackerman, S. (1996) Altruism, Nonprofits, and Economic Theory, *Journal of Economic Literature*, 34(2), pp.701–728.

RSC (n.d.) We Are To Conclude Our Partnership With BP, *RSC* website, accessed 20 March 2021.

Sainato, M. (2020) 'I'm Not A Robot': Amazon Workers Condemn Unsafe, Gruelling Conditions At Warehouse, 5 February 2020.

Salway, M. (2020) Interviewed by Mitchell, S. (30 November 2020).

Sanders, M. and Tamma, F. (2015) The Science Behind Why People Give Money To Charity, The Guardian Labs, 23 March 2015.

Scharf, K. (2014) More Tax Incentives Needed To Weed Out Inefficient 'Warm-Glow' Charities, Warwick University website, 2 July 2014.

Sheil, F. and Breidenbach-Roe, R. (2014) Payment by Results and the Voluntary Sector, NCVO, April 2014.

Sheila McKechnie Foundation (2017) The Chilling Reality: How the Lobbying Act is Affecting Charity & Voluntary Sector Campaigning in the UK, Sheila McKechnie Foundation.

Shelter (2004) Off the Streets: Tackling Homelessness Among Female Streetbased Sex Workers, Shelter.

Shelter (2021) What We Do, Shelter website, 20 March 2021.

Skills Platform et al. (2020) The Charity Digital Skills Report, Skills Platform and Zoe Amar Digital.

Sky Sports (2020) Sir Andrew Strauss Blown Away After Ruth Strauss Foundation Donations Exceed £870,000, Sky Sports, 29 July 2020.

Smith, J.D. (2019) 100 Years of NCVO and Voluntary Action: Idealists and Realists, Springer.

Sodha, S. (2016) The Future of Doing Good in the UK, National Lottery.

Sparkes, J. (2020) Interviewed Mitchell, S. (16 January 2020).

Sproson, K. (2020) Cheap and Free Wills: Low-cost Ways to Write Your Will, Money Saving Expert website, 13 November 2020.

Starr, K. and Coussa, G. (2018) Enough Innovation Already! Innovation Without Replication Is A Waste Of Time, Stanford Social Innovation Review, 6 April 2018.

Stonewall (2021) Mission and Vision, Stonewall website, 20 March 2021.

Szreter, S. and Ishkanian, A. (2012) Introduction: What is Big Society? Contemporary Social Policy in a Historical and Comparative Perspective. In The Big Society Debate. Edward Elgar Publishing.

Taylor, M. (2020) The Evolution of Extinction Rebellion, The Guardian, 4 August 2020.

Thoreau, H.D. (1854) Walden, Yale University Press.

Thorne, J. (2020) Interviewed Mitchell, S. (10 June 2020).

Tiratelli, L. and Kaye, S. (2020) Communities Vs Coronavirus: The Rise Of New Mutual Aid, New Local Government Association.

Townsend, M. (2019) Tube Protest Was A Mistake, Admit Leading Extinction Rebellion Members, The Guardian, 20 October 2019.

Unwin, J. (2004) The Grantmaking Tango: Issues for Funders, Barings Foundation.

Unwin, J. (2019) Voluntary Trustees: Are We Paying A Price for This Principle? Julia Unwin website, 3 June 2019.

Volunteering England (2003) Volunteers and the Law, Volunteering England.

Wallis, L. (2019) Bullying In The Voluntary Sector: 'I Was Effectively Outed At Work', Guardian Society, 6 February 2019.

Weaver, M. (2019) Daily Mail Pays Charity Damages Over 'Hate Festival' Allegations, The Guardian, 13 June 2019.

Weymouth, L. (2019) RSPCA Accused of Pushing Away Staff Amid 'Bullying and Retention Crises', Charity Times, 30 October 2019.

Whelan, T. and Kronthal-Sacco, R. (2019) Research: Actually, Customers Do Buy Sustainable Products, Harvard Business Review, 19 June 2019.

Whitehead, R. (2019) One Quarter of the Top Charity CEOs Went to Oxbridge, *Civil Society*, 21 November 2019.

Whitehead, H. (2020) Charity Commission Chair Warns Charities Not To Engage In 'Culture Wars', Civil Society, 30 November 2020.

Wilkins, C. (2020) Is The Future Unrestricted? Charity Funding Post Covid-19?, *NPC blog*, 10 June 2020.

Wilson, P. (2020) *Interviewed Mitchell, S.* (12 June 2020).

World Economic Forum (2018) *Operating Models for the Future of Consumption, Insight Report*, World Economic Forum.

INDEX

Printed in Great Britain
by Amazon